Healthy urban planning

Healthy urban planning means planning for people. It promotes the idea that a city is much more than buildings, streets and open spaces: a living, breathing organism, the health of which is closely linked to that of its citizens.

It has long been acknowledged that conditions in cities, sometimes compounded by urban planning practices, can be detrimental to health. *Healthy urban planning* focuses on the positive effects that urban planning can have on human health, wellbeing and quality of life and reflects WHO's broad definition of health. The book explains concepts and principles and draws on the experiences of cities and towns throughout Europe, many of which are part of the Healthy Cities movement. It then goes on to suggest an approach that puts a desire for healthy citizens back at the very heart of urban planning practice.

Professionals involved in planning, designing and regenerating the urban environment will find the ideas and approaches contained in this book refreshing and stimulating. It will also enable public health professionals to learn more about the role urban planners can play in promoting health.

Hugh Barton is an urban planner and Executive Director of the WHO Collaborating Centre for Healthy Cities and Urban Policy at the University of the West of England. **Catherine Tsourou** is a freelance architect and urban planner based in Padua, Italy. Both authors have been involved in WHO's developmental work on healthy urban planning carried out as part of the Healthy Cities project.

Routledge
Taylor & Francis Group

LONDON AND NEW YORK

Healthy urban planning

A WHO guide to planning for people

Hugh Barton and Catherine Tsourou

Routledge
Taylor & Francis Group

LONDON AND NEW YORK

Published on behalf of the
World Health Organization
Regional Office for Europe
by Spon Press

First published 2000 by Spon Press
11 New Fetter Lane, London EC4P 4EE
on behalf of the World Health Organization

Simultaneously published in the USA and Canada
by Spon Press
29 West 35th Street, New York, NY 10001
on behalf of the World Health Organization

Spon Press is an imprint of the Taylor & Francis Group

© 2000 World Health Organization

Text editing: David Breuer

This edition published 2011 by Routledge
2 Park Square, Milton Park, Abingdon, Oxon OX14 4RN
711 Third Avenue, New York, NY 10017, USA
Routledge is an imprint of the Taylor & Francis Group, an informa business

British Library Cataloguing in Publication Data
A catalogue record for this book is available from the British Library.

Library of Congress Cataloguing in Publication Data
A catalogue record for this book has been requested.

ISBN 978 0 4152 4327 8

Contents

Tables

Figures

Foreword

The urban planning movement, like the public health movement, evolved as a response to conditions in the rapidly expanding cities of nineteenth-century Europe. The effects of poor-quality and unsanitary housing on the health of factory workers supporting the growing industrial economy gave rise to a new group of professions concerned with improving the health and quality of life of citizens. Much has happened in urban planning and public health since those early days, and we now know much more about the determinants of health. Nevertheless, since that time, the links between urban planning and health have become increasingly undervalued, ignored and perhaps even forgotten. The planning systems of Europe have focused more and more on the built environment as a means to achieve a narrowly defined version of an efficient city, promoting short-term financial gain to the detriment of the inhabitants. The health and quality of life of the citizens need to be given priority throughout Europe. This should not be an afterthought or a peripheral activity but an approach compatible with sustainable economic growth, where the needs of a city's people are truly at the centre of urban planning.

The concept of healthy urban planning has been developed as part of the WHO Healthy Cities project, a longstanding programme that addresses all aspects of health in the urban context. Urban planning practices in common with cities themselves can affect the health of individual citizens both positively and negatively. The links are complex and have many dimensions, including social, environmental and economic. Healthy urban planning focuses on the positive aspects. It aims to refocus urban planners on the implications of their work for human health and wellbeing and, in particular, to make health objectives central to the decision-making process. In this way it places people at the very centre of the urban planning agenda. Health is a core element of sustainable development, and healthy urban planning aims to improve both the quality of the built environment and the quality of life of individuals and communities in cities. It can help to create a healthy economy, a healthy environment and a healthy society.

Marc Danzon
WHO Regional Director for Europe

Acknowledgements

Healthy urban planning is the result of a collaboration between the Centre for Urban Health of the WHO Regional Office for Europe, the WHO Collaborating Centre for Healthy Cities and Urban Policy at the University of the West of England, Bristol and the Institute of Architecture at the University of Venice. We thank the following people for their role as supporting authors and their valuable contributions in the drafting process: Jim Claydon and Isobel Daniels (University of the West of England) and Guiseppe Longhi (University of Venice).

Thanks are due to the City of Milan, hosts of the WHO Seminar on Healthy Urban Planning held in October 1999 at which a preliminary version of this book was discussed, and the participants for their comments and contributions during the Seminar. Thanks also go to Claire Mitcham (focal point for urban planning at the WHO Centre for Urban Health) for coordinating, editing, and guiding the production of this document.

The following people have provided much appreciated input into this book by giving comments and suggestions on earlier drafts: Roderick Lawrence (University of Geneva), Pierre Dubé (National Capital Commission for Canada), Julia Muschner (Dresden Healthy City Project), Batya Waschitz (Jerusalem Healthy City Project), Hank Van Tilborg (Planning Department, City of Rotterdam), Eva Stankova (Planning Department, City of Brno), Bjarne Gregersen (Planning Department, Municipality of Horsens), Robert Pedersen (6 a day project, Copenhagen), and Aileen Robertson and Xavier Bonnefoy (WHO Regional Office for Europe). A special word of thanks goes to Anne Mette Nielsen for her excellent assistance and for typesetting this book. Finally, many thanks to David Breuer, who significantly improved the language and style of this book.

Introduction

The condition of the urban environment and how it is managed and used by its inhabitants are fundamental to human health and wellbeing. Many of the problems in cities today relate to poor residential and other environments, poverty, inequity, pollution, unemployment, lack of access to jobs, goods and services, and lack of community cohesion. Urban planners influence the social, physical and economic environments and how cities function. They therefore have a key role to play in addressing these problems and securing conditions in cities conducive to health and wellbeing and a high quality of life.

Urban planning makes decisions about the use and development of land and buildings in cities. It has evolved throughout Europe, as a way to ensure that these decisions are taken with the public interest in mind. A variety of names for this process have emerged in different European countries as a result of the various legislative and institutional processes within which urban planners work. These terms were identified by the European Commission *(1)* and include: spatial planning, land-use planning, town and country planning, physical planning, urban and regional planning, territorial planning and space management systems.

Healthy urban planning highlights the importance of recognizing the health implications of policy and practice in urban planning and the need to go one step further, by pursuing health objectives as a central part of urban planning work. Healthy urban planning is a concept that has evolved through the work of the Healthy Cities movement. In Europe, the third phase of the WHO Healthy Cities project (1998–2002) is developing healthy urban planning principles and practices as a priority. The aim is to show that urban planning principles are closely aligned with the Healthy Cities approach to urban management and to refocus urban planning on health and the quality of life. If cities are to become healthy and attractive places to live in the future, it is vital that urban planners in every country focus on people and how they use buildings and developments, rather than simply on the buildings themselves, as has become the case in many of our cities. Duhl & Sanchez *(2)* highlighted the historical links between urban planning and health. The complexities of urban life and urban problems make it essential to relearn why the links between health and urban planning are of key importance in cities and to act accordingly.

This book forms part of the developmental work on healthy urban planning of the Centre for Urban Health of the WHO Regional Office for Europe, and its form and content has evolved as part of that work. The draft text was the subject of the WHO Seminar on Healthy Urban Planning in Milan, Italy, in October 1999, at which urban planners from across Europe discussed the issues and explored ways of taking WHO's initiative forward. The book complements and builds on previous publications and documents related to urban planning produced by the Regional Office *(2–8)*. It is not intended to be definitive nor to provide all the answers but to help to stimulate and inform the debate on healthy urban planning.

The authors do not seek to examine the differences between urban planning systems in Europe. Numerous commentators have done this *(8–11)*. Instead, the book illustrates why urban planning should bring the consideration of health effects into the heart of the decision-making process. Since planning systems and techniques across Europe sometimes differ quite widely, every country and every city must find the most appropriate ways to implement the concept of healthy urban planning. The aim is therefore to provide assistance to urban planners in integrating health more fully into their decision-making processes.

This book is intended to be used by professionals working in a variety of disciplines that contribute to urban planning: land-use and town planners, architects, developers, urban designers, transport planners and people working on the regeneration, renewal and economic development of urban areas. It will also appeal to academics and students in those professions. Finally, it will enable public health professionals to learn more about the role of urban planners in improving the health of citizens. Reading the whole book provides a comprehensive picture of healthy urban planning, but readers can also return to the book again and again, dipping into different sections to refer to conceptual issues, guidance and case studies as the need arises.

Part one introduces the concept of healthy urban planning. Chapter 1 presents WHO's definition of health, whereby health is not merely the absence of disease but includes human wellbeing and quality of life. It outlines the links between health and urban planning and defines the health objectives of planning. Chapter 2 describes the unique value of the Healthy Cities approach to urban management, showing why the movement is relevant to urban planners. Chapter 3 goes on to discuss the extent to which healthy urban planning has become a reality in cities participating in the WHO Healthy Cities project since 1987, providing viewpoints and case studies from a recent survey. Part two of the book gives detailed advice on how to plan in healthy ways at different levels. Chapter 4 describes strategies for an entire city or urban region. A clear strategy for urban form is recommended that considers the location of jobs and facilities, housing provision and density, integrated transport planning and planning for key resources. Chapter 5 translates the principles of healthy urban planning to the neighbourhood level, arguing that communities should have greater power over the decision-making processes that affect their neighbourhood. In chapter 6, a series of checklists is provided that are intended to assist in assessing the compatibility of new development sites and proposals with the principles of healthy urban planning. Case studies are provided throughout the book.

Part one

Concepts, principles and practice

Part one introduces the concept of healthy urban planning. Chapter 1 presents WHO's definition of health, whereby health is not merely the absence of disease but includes human wellbeing and quality of life. It outlines the links between health and urban planning and defines the health objectives of planning. Chapter 2 describes the unique value of the Healthy Cities approach to urban management, showing why the movement is relevant to urban planners. Chapter 3 discusses the extent to which healthy urban planning has become a reality in cities participating in the WHO Healthy Cities project since 1987, providing viewpoints and case studies from a recent survey.

Chapter 1

The links between health and urban planning

THE CONCEPT OF HEALTH

> Health is a state of complete physical, mental and social well-being and not merely the absence of disease or infirmity. The enjoyment of the highest attainable standard of health is one of the fundamental rights of every human being, without distinction of race, religion, political belief, economic or social condition.

The above definition of health, formulated in the Constitution of the World Health Organization (1946), challenges the conventional assumption that health policy is a matter only for health care professionals. This chapter argues that health should be a central goal of many professions and agencies, and specifically, that urban planners have a key role in promoting a healthy environment. It has taken a long time for the change in consciousness encompassed in the WHO definition of health to be consolidated in practice; indeed, it was not until the late 1970s that the traditional research focus on pathogenesis (the cause of diseases) was integrated with research into salutogenesis (discovering the causes of health and acting to strengthen them). Many urban planning systems do not encompass health issues. Yet the quality of the environment and the nature of development are major determinants of health. Health in turn is an important stimulus to economic productivity. Health is about the quality of life experienced by people now, but planning for health implies a concern for future generations. Lifestyle and household decisions shape health, but these decisions are constrained by the economic and social opportunities, income, education and quality of the environment experienced by the household's members.

Various descriptive and interrelational models have been developed to explain the relationship between health and the total environment (biological, physical, social and economic). Fig. 1.1 helps to illustrate the links between the determinant factors of health and is well documented within WHO literature.

Fig. 1.1.   The factors determining health

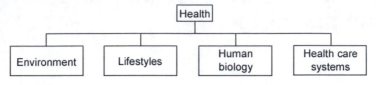

Source: Lalonde *(12)*

The model by Whitehead & Dahlgren *(13)* illustrated in Fig. 1.2 elaborates further and, in addition to identifying the factors influencing health, describes the four levels or strata of influence.

- In the centre are individuals with their predetermined genetic heritage, surrounded by influences on health that can be modified.
- The first stratum concerns personal behaviour and lifestyle, influenced by models of friendship and community regulations that may promote or damage health.
- The second stratum includes social and community influences: the availability or lack of reciprocal support in unfavourable conditions with consequent positive or negative effects.
- The third stratum incorporates structural factors such as housing and working conditions and access to services and facilities.
- The fourth stratum incorporates the factors that influence society as a whole: these include socioeconomic, cultural and environmental conditions.

Fig. 1.2.   The main determinants of health

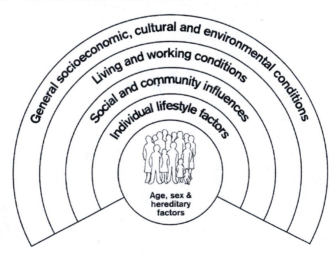

Source: Whitehead & Dahlgren *(13)*

Fig. 1.3.   The health gradient

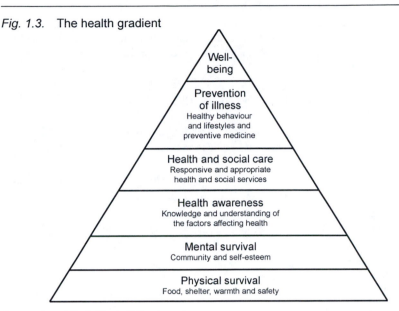

Source: Laughlin & Black *(14)*

Fig. 1.3 illustrates the interaction of a range of health factors in society, represented as a health gradient. This implies that the slope of the health gradient varies according to socioeconomic background and that certain groups may be subject to a greater degree of poor health. Promoting health based solely on changing the traditional behaviour of the individual may have little impact on people who are less advantaged. This requires action from outside.

Good health or wellbeing are achieved through a number of stages, as set out in Fig. 1.3. The activity marked at the top of the triangle will not lead to good health without an activity that also concentrates on the lower levels, and the equilibrium of activity must reflect the characteristics of the local community. The interrelationship and mutual influence of all these factors means that any action to improve health must cover all the levels of the hierarchy at the same time.

THE EFFECTS OF URBAN PLANNING ON HEALTH

Urban planning refers to the institutionalized process of making decisions about the future use and character of land and buildings in city regions. Mechanisms to ensure that these decisions are taken in the public interest have evolved throughout Europe and differ according to a number of factors. These factors were recognized by the WHO Regional Office for Europe in 1999 *(8)*:

The type of planning system that has evolved in each European country has depended on the country's legal system and institutional framework, the relative roles of the different actors in the development process and the degree to which a separate planning profession has emerged.

A number of texts on both planning systems and governance in Europe are available, and the similarities and differences between countries are thoroughly examined within these *(3–5,8–11)*. Although urban planning systems may vary in different countries, the concepts, principles and goals that underpin those systems have much in common.

The prevalence of the medical model of health, which focuses on the individual and the treatment of illness and dominated the latter part of the twentieth century, is beginning to shift to the social model, in which health is the result of a series of socioeconomic, cultural and environmental factors, housing conditions, employment and community. Urban plans are prepared for physical development, but the goals of these plans are essentially social. Urban planning policy therefore significantly influences health throughout Europe.

The idea that health and urban planning are linked is not new *(2)*. Indeed, in many European countries town planning originated early in the twentieth century as a result of consensual concerns about the health and housing of citizens. In the nineteenth century, the need to put an end to the epidemics rife in industrialized urban areas led to a close interconnection between public health and urban planning. This theme is being taken up again a century later.

These concerns were originally expressed in terms of space and infrastructure standards being established for housing and simple forms of land-use zoning. From this reactive approach emerged the more active form of intervention through making urban plans with the aim of establishing basic standards of provision within new development, using an approach that was also based on estimating and providing for the future needs of communities.

Many of the effects of urban planning decisions on the health of the population are ignored in contemporary planning practice, although there is great concern for specific aspects of health, such as road safety. Yet a careful analysis shows profound effects on all the levels of influence on individual health identified by Whitehead & Dahlgren (Fig. 1.2) *(2,13)*. It is not simply a matter of accidents and road traffic policy. Rather the social goal of health can be a fundamental justification for and purpose of urban planning. A book produced as part of WHO's campaign on the social determinants of health *(15)* examines these determinants in detail. *The solid facts: social determinants of health (16)* examines policy and action for health geared towards addressing these issues.

Table 1.1 sets out the relationship between the main planning policy areas and relevant determinants of health. The determinants are organized by level (Fig. 1.2); all levels, from lifestyle choices to broad environmental variables, are affected.

Individual behaviour and lifestyle. The first level of influence is individual behaviour and lifestyle. The physical environment, which is shaped by planning decisions, can facilitate or deter a healthy lifestyle. The propensity of people to walk, cycle or play in the open air is affected by the convenience, quality and safety of pedestrian and cycling routes and by the availability of local open space. This is critically important in relation to children, as the habit of healthy regular exercise is formed or not formed during childhood and lasts a lifetime. Regular exercise "protects against heart disease and, by limiting obesity, reduces the onset of diabetes. It promotes a sense of wellbeing and protects older people from depression" *(16)*.

Social and community influences. The second level of influence on personal health includes social and community influences: urban planning can act to destroy social networks, as in insensitive urban renewal schemes, or can conversely cultivate opportunities for a rich community life. Local networks of mutual support and friendships are affected by the existence of common activities and meeting places: schools, post offices, pubs and convivial, safe streets. The sustaining of such local facilities and networks depends in part on coherent long-term strategies for housing, economic development and transport. Social support is particularly important for the most vulnerable groups. Without it people are "likely to experience less wellbeing, more depression, greater risk of pregnancy complications and higher levels of disability from chronic diseases" *(16)*. This does not mean that urban planning can "create" communities. It is people who choose to form communities. But planning affects the opportunities they have to choose.

Local structural conditions. At the third level of influence – local structural conditions – planning policy very directly affects personal health in a number of ways. For example, the lack of sufficient housing of adequate quality can lead to housing stress and fuel poverty, which affect health; accessible work opportunities can help alleviate poverty and depression and consequently the poor health caused by unemployment; and an accessible urban structure together with an efficient, inexpensive transport system can reduce problems of social exclusion and open up opportunities for poor and less mobile people.

General socioeconomic, cultural and environmental conditions. At the broadest level of influence, local urban planning affects the quality of air, water and soil resources. It also affects the emission of greenhouse gases, particularly in buildings and transport, and thus acts to exacerbate or mitigate the health risks of rapid climate change.

Table 1.1. Matrix of planning policy areas and the social and environmental determinants of health

Level (see Fig. 1.2)	Determinants of health	Building regulations	Housing policy	Economic development	Social services and benefits	Open space	Transport	Energy, water and drainage	Urban form	Urban regeneration
1	Personal lifestyles		*	*	*	**	**		*	*
2	Social cohesion		*	*	*	*	*		**	*
3	Housing	**	**	**					*	*
3	Work	*	**	*	**		*	**	*	*
3	Access	**	*	*		*	**		**	*
3	Food	*				*			*	
3	Safety	*	**	*			**		*	*
3	Equity	*	**		**	*	**	*	**	*
4	Air quality and aesthetics	*	*	**		*	**	*	*	*
4	Water and sanitation	**		*		*		**		
4	Soil and solid waste	*		*		*				**
4	Global climate	**	*	**	*	*	**	**	**	*

Planning policy areas

Source: adapted from Barton et al. (*17*)

Planning is defined in terms of the development of land and buildings and towns. This chart does not therefore highlight the subsequent regulation of levels of pollution and other factors. Nor does it focus on the social, education and health services *per se* but rather their accessibility.

* Important influences on health

** Critical or prime influences on health

Table 1.1 shows that all the major aspects of planning policy influence health outcome. It also serves to stress that planning and health are not related in any simple linear way. Improving any facet of health requires coordinated action across a wide range of policy areas. Furthermore, action solely in the sphere of the physical environment is never sufficient. It needs to be compatible with and help reinforce action in other social and economic policy arenas through a partnership approach.

TWELVE KEY HEALTH OBJECTIVES FOR PLANNERS

Boxes 1.1 to 1.12 transform the 12 key determinants of health from Table 1.1 into health objectives for planners and criteria for assessing policy. The potential health benefits are spelled out in each case, together with a brief indication of appropriate and inappropriate policies.

Box 1.1.   Twelve key health objectives for planners: healthy lifestyles

Criteria for assessing policy	Do planning policies and proposals encourage and promote healthy exercise?
Health benefits	Healthy exercise combats heart disease, strokes and other diseases that are associated with both sedentary occupations and stressful lifestyles. Healthy lifestyles can improve mental wellbeing and therefore influence physical health.
Potential negative effects of planning	Low-density housing and providing facilities that lead to longer trip patterns and encourage excessive use of cars do not encourage healthy lifestyles.
Positive effects of planning	Planning can create attractive, safe and convenient environments that encourage people to walk or cycle to work, shop, school and other local facilities. Development plans can ensure adequate recreational opportunities with equality of distribution among the community and in suitably accessible locations.

Box 1.2.   Twelve key health objectives for planners: social cohesion

Criteria for assessing policy	Do planning policies and proposals encourage and promote social cohesion?
Health benefits	Friendship and supportive networks throughout the community can help the individual at home and at work to speed recovery after illness and reduce depression and chronic illness. This can lead to greater fulfilment. Fragmentation of the social structure can lead to ghettos according to socioeconomic status, age and race, and this can lead to isolation and insecurity.
Potential negative effects of planning	Social cohesion can be undermined by insensitive housing redevelopment and dispersal of resident communities. It is also undermined by roads severing community links and constructing barriers to pedestrian connectivity and by large, intimidating commercial schemes.
Positive effects of planning	Urban planning cannot create local community or cohesive social networks. However, social cohesion can be facilitated by creating safe and permeable environments with natural social foci where people can meet informally. Mixed-use development in town centres and commercial environments as well as residential neighbourhoods can help widen social options.

Box 1.3.   Twelve key health objectives for planners: housing quality

Criteria for assessing policy	Do planning policies and proposals encourage and promote housing quality?
Health benefits	Access to adequate housing is critically important, especially for very young and old people. The health

effects of early development last a lifetime. Environmental factors and lack of hygiene and sanitation in buildings and urban spaces have been widely recognized as causing illness since the dawn of urban planning.

Potential negative effects of planning

Insufficient, overcrowded housing built with toxic materials and unsafe structures is detrimental to physical health. Overcrowding is associated with mental disorders, physical illness and accidents. Poor choice of location, design and orientation of housing developments can exacerbate incidents of crime and vandalism. Very tall residential buildings can affect mental health, and combined with social isolation can lead to depression and ill health *(2)*.

Positive effects of planning

Housing quality can be improved by ensuring that detailed design, orientation and appropriate energy-efficient materials are used in construction, with siting to reduce heat loss. Providing a sufficient range of housing tenure with good basic services is essential. Adaptable buildings can be planned for community uses such as health, education and leisure.

Box 1.4. Twelve key health objectives for planners: access to work

Criteria for assessing policy

Do planning policies and proposals encourage and promote access to employment opportunities?

Health benefits

Job security can increase health, wellbeing and job satisfaction. Unemployed people suffer an increased risk of financial stress, which can lead to ill health, mental problems and even premature death.

Potential negative effects of planning

Planning can frustrate or facilitate the provision of job opportunities. Employment opportunities created in inaccessible locations or a lack of a variety of jobs in a community can negatively affect health both directly and indirectly.

Positive effects of planning

Urban planning, linked to strategies for economic regeneration, can assist by facilitating attractive opportunities for business and can encourage diversity in employment and ensure that local job opportunities are retained. Equitable transport strategies can also play an important part in providing access to job opportunities. The provision of local work opportunities can encourage shorter trip lengths and thus reduce emissions from transport.

Box 1.5.   Twelve key health objectives for planners: accessibility

Criteria for assessing policy

Do planning policies and proposals encourage and promote accessibility?

Health benefits

Reducing dependence on cars and motorized forms of travel can lead to more physical exercise and reduce levels of heart disease and other chronic illnesses. A growing number of children miss out on the regular exercise of getting to school, and at the same time concerns about obesity are growing. The patterns of physical activity established in childhood are perceived to be a key determinant of adult behaviour *(18).*

Potential negative effects of planning

In many countries, public services such as hospitals and schools are being rationalized, leading to the closure of facilities. This has transferred the responsibility for travel to the individual. This can restrict access, leading to disadvantage for certain specific groups in the community, such as elderly people, women, children, handicapped people and ethnic minorities. Bulk shopping facilities located out of town have also increased car dependence, often to the detriment of local facilities.

Positive effects of planning	Planning can improve the choice of different transport modes available, in particular by making local facilities more accessible to people walking, cycling and using public transport. Safe and environmentally sound cycling and walking networks can be promoted and traffic managed to slow, calm and reduce vehicle speeds in residential areas.

Box 1.6.   Twelve key health objectives for planners: local, low-input food production

Criteria for assessing policy	Do planning policies and proposals encourage and promote local food production with low input of chemical fertilizer and pesticides?
Health benefits	Social gradients in the quality of diet and sources of nutrients contribute to inequality in health through the excessive consumption of energy-dense fat and sugar. Dietary goals to prevent chronic disease consistently emphasize the need to eat more fresh fruit and vegetables. People on low incomes, including young families, elderly people and unemployed people, are the least able to eat well. Growing and distributing food locally can promote mental health by increasing levels of physical activity, reducing social isolation and improving self-esteem and confidence.
Potential negative effects of planning	Planning can overlook the importance of accessible open spaces and providing local allotment gardens. The centralization of shopping facilities and growth of large supermarkets reduces the variety of food available locally and disadvantages those without access to car transport, which exacerbates social inequity.
Positive effects of planning	Local food sources such as market gardens, allotment gardens, smallholdings and city farms can enable

people on low incomes to grow their own fruit and vegetables. New healthy living centres are developing such initiatives on site to combine opportunities for health and wellbeing with gentle exercise. Urban planning can assist by preserving and protecting areas for small-scale community projects and opportunities for local food production. Urban planning can also encourage a diversity of shopping facilities in local centres, helping to alleviate individual reliance on large supermarkets outside town centres *(19)*.

Box 1.7. Twelve key health objectives for planners: safety

Criteria for assessing policy	Do planning policies and proposals encourage and promote safety and the feeling of safety in the community?
Health benefits	The biggest cause of accidents is road traffic, with the most vulnerable groups, including young, elderly and disabled people, being particularly at risk. Accidents in and around the home are also the greatest single threat to life for children and young people.
Potential negative effects of planning	Urban planning can do much to worsen or alienate the problems of safety on the streets. A sense of safety on the street includes freedom from assault and from the fear of assault. Where the local pedestrian environment is intimidating and inconvenient, people use cars, and social interaction is reduced *(2)*.
Positive effects of planning	Traffic-calming techniques to slow the speed of road traffic and give priority to pedestrians and cyclists are key to a safer environment. The detailed design and layout of residential and commercial areas can ensure a natural process of surveillance over public

space that reduces both the fear of and the actual incidence of crime.

Box 1.8. Twelve key health objectives for planners: equity

Criteria for assessing policy	Do planning policies and proposals encourage and promote equity and the development of social capital?
Health benefits	Poor health and premature death can be reduced by cutting levels of poverty. The harm to health comes not only from material deprivation but also from the social and psychological problems of living in poverty *(16).*
Potential negative effects of planning	Planning does not directly affect income but does have many indirect effects. The planning system can be used, for example, to hinder or to help the process of providing a range of facilities and providing opportunities for improving levels of equity.
Positive effects of planning	The planning system can help in the process of providing social or low-cost housing; it can facilitate the provision of job opportunities; and through its influence on the safety and convenience of neighbourhoods, can improve patterns of movement by providing a range of easily accessible facilities. Local networks of mutual support are enhanced by these factors, with can help foster a sense of local community.

Box 1.9. Twelve key health objectives for planners: air quality and aesthetics

Criteria for assessing policy	Do planning policies and proposals encourage and promote good air quality, protection from excessive

	noise and an attractive environment for living and working?
Health benefits	The health benefits of improved air quality include a reduced incidence of severe lung diseases (chronic bronchitis or emphysema) and heart conditions and, probably, reduced levels of asthma among children. An attractive environment increases people's sense of wellbeing.
Potential negative effects of planning	Poor air quality results in part from ineffective land-use and transport strategies leading to high levels of road traffic and factories polluting residential areas. The absence of good-neighbour policies can mean that residents and workers are subject to excessive noise, unpleasant fumes and visually arid environments that can undermine wellbeing and contribute to illness.
Positive effects of planning	Planning can assist by putting local environmental quality high on the agenda in commercial and industrial areas as well as residential ones; by segregating polluting and noisy industrial uses of land; by promoting less polluting forms of public transport, deterring car use and restricting lorries to specific routes; and by supporting the development of energy-efficient buildings and neighbourhoods.

Box 1.10. Twelve key health objectives for planners: water and sanitation quality

Criteria for assessing policy	Do planning policies and proposals encourage and promote improved water and sanitation quality?
Health benefits	Good water quality and sanitation are critical to health and preventing disease.

Potential negative effects of planning	Planning may only indirectly affect water supply and wastewater treatment, but health can be adversely affected if the use of local sourcing and local treatment of supplies is not encouraged.
Positive effects of planning	Urban planning can impose standards and criteria that any new development has to meet. It can promote on-site water collection, purification and infiltration back into the ground or replenishing streams. It can aim to ensure that development does not take place where there is a threat from flooding and that aquifers are not contaminated when agricultural, transport and industrial processes are planned.

Box 1.11.   Twelve key health objectives for planners: quality of
                 land and mineral resources

Criteria for assessing policy	Do planning policies and proposals encourage and promote the conservation and quality of land and mineral resources?
Health benefits	Reducing contamination by industrial waste or by ineffective waste management and tipping can greatly improve human health and the quality of the environment.
Potential negative effects of planning	Planning cannot always influence this but can raise awareness that land degradation can be caused by excessively intensive agriculture and deforestation as well as excessive use of mineral resources in infrastructure projects. Planners can try to ensure that development is avoided on prime agricultural land with high-grade soil.
Positive effects of planning	Planning can ensure that recycled and renewable materials are used whenever possible in the building construction process. New building types can be

encouraged that incorporate composting and growing food. Urban open spaces and local allotment gardens, market gardens, smallholdings and food-growing activities on the urban fringe can be safeguarded. Brownfield sites or derelict urban land can be redeveloped *(4)*.

Box 1.12.   Twelve key health objectives for planners: climate stability

Criteria for assessing policy
Do planning policies and proposals encourage and promote climate stability?

Health benefits
A reduction in extremes of temperature may prevent death among deprived groups and elderly people. If disease and sea-level rises associated with climate instability can be prevented, fewer people will become ill or displaced from their homes.

Potential negative effects of planning
Planning can contribute to climatic problems by failing to consider policies that encourage reductions in fossil fuel use, including energy conservation in the construction and use of buildings *(2,20)*.

Positive effects of planning
Urban planning can affect the rate of human emissions of greenhouse gases by influencing energy use in buildings and transport and by developing renewable energy sources.

THE NEED FOR HEALTHY URBAN PLANNING

The health objectives of urban planning described above illustrate how, by influencing a variety of conditions in cities, urban planning can either promote or damage health and the quality of life. Healthy urban planning involves planning practices that promote health and wellbeing and has much in common with the principles of sustainable development. It means focusing on humans and how they use their environments in planning rather than simply concentrating on buildings and economics.

Healthy urban planning implies a need to place values such as equity and collaboration (including intersectoral cooperation and community participation) at the centre of the decision-making process; these themes are explored throughout this book and form key values in WHO's policy for health for all, which is introduced in the next chapter.

In promoting equity, central to healthy urban planning is a need to implement policies aimed at improving the living standards of disadvantaged and vulnerable populations and to bear in mind the diversity of city users in terms of age, gender, physical ability, ethnic origin and economic circumstances. Putting the principle of equity at the heart of urban planning practices reduces the imbalance in the urban fabric and problems associated with access to transport, air and noise pollution and increases the quality of public spaces, social cohesion, healthy lifestyles and employment opportunities.

In most cases, urban planning agencies are not the only body or even necessarily the main body responsible for the factors related to the health objectives of urban planning, and collaboration is therefore essential. Other social, economic and environmental organizations are involved. In this situation a collaborative approach, working in partnership towards agreed objectives, is essential. Collaboration in urban planning involves both different approaches to decision-making and conscious attempts to engage the community. Part of the process requires identifying the stakeholders in the community who hold competing interests in decisions *(2)*.

Duhl & Sanchez *(2)* summarize Luke's *(21)* idea of stakeholders and their relationship to urban planners in developing the healthy city:

> Healthy urban planning does not view multiculturalism and diversity as problems to be overcome but rather as rich opportunities waiting to be seized. Urban planning must be sustained by dynamic leadership styles and open to various configurations. For example, it should be open to collaborative and bottom-up actions. Healthy urban planning thus makes room for citizens as leaders and requires catalytic leadership from planners. Planners become effective public leaders when they serve as catalysts who reach beyond the traditional boundaries to engage, discuss and mediate among broad groups of stakeholders.

The ideas and principles central to healthy urban planning can be implemented throughout Europe, regardless of the differences in urban planning systems. It is important to remember from the outset, however, that differences do exist, and each country and city needs to find ways to implement the concept that best responds to their individual circumstances.

The WHO Healthy Cities project emphasizes promoting healthy urban planning as a core aspect of Healthy Cities work. The following chapters examine the background and content of the Healthy Cities approach to urban management. They provide an overview of the Healthy Cities movement in Europe and outline the relationship between the work of healthy city projects and urban planners, illustrating the need for urban planners to take a role in creating healthy cities.

Healthy Cities networks throughout Europe and around the world provide a framework and the support to promote healthy urban planning, but any city can and should put health objectives at the heart of its decision-making process and make healthy urban planning a reality.

Chapter 2

The Healthy Cities project and urban planning

INTRODUCTION

This chapter outlines the Healthy Cities approach to urban management. It begins by outlining the background, origin and evolution of the Healthy Cities movement within the context of the WHO strategy for health for all. It then examines the key principles of healthy cities and relates these to the ethics and values of urban planning, highlighting the implications for practice. Finally, the practical aspects of the Healthy Cities approach, what it involves and how it affects organizational and working practices are explained. The benefits of this approach for urban planners, the importance of involving urban planners in Healthy Cities work and the opportunities for healthy urban planning are demonstrated.

HEALTH FOR ALL

During the 1970s, people worldwide became increasingly dissatisfied with the inability of existing health services to respond to newly emerging health requirements and expectations. The Member States of WHO commissioned the Organization to develop a programme of public health reform.

The resulting strategy for health for all by the year 2000 (22) was launched at the World Health Assembly in 1979. It highlighted the idea that the main areas where action was needed to improve health and wellbeing lay outside the health sector.

In 1998 the Member States of WHO adopted an updated strategy for health for all in the twenty-first century (23) and supported this with a World Health Declaration. The Member States of the European Region subsequently endorsed a new health for all policy framework for the European Region, HEALTH21 (24), which sets out 21 targets for the twenty-first century (Annex 1). The goal of this new policy is to achieve full health potential for all. Its three basic values are:

- health as a fundamental human right;
- equity in health and solidarity in action between countries, between groups of people within countries and between genders; and
- participation by and accountability of individuals, groups and communities and of institutions, organizations and sectors in health development.

Four strategies for action were chosen "to ensure that scientific, economic, social and political sustainability drive the implementation of HEALTH21":

- multisectoral strategies to tackle the determinants of health, taking into account physical, economic, social, cultural, and gender perspectives and ensuring the use of health impact assessments;
- health-outcome-driven programmes and investments for health development and clinical care;
- integrated family- and community-oriented primary health care, supported by a flexible and responsive hospital system; and
- a participatory health development process that involves relevant partners for health, at all levels – home, school and worksite, local community and country – and that promotes joint decision-making, implementation and accountability.

The Ottawa Charter for Health Promotion *(25)* was adopted at the First International Conference on Health Promotion in 1986. It built on the policy of health for all and highlighted the need to promote health, recognizing that building healthier societies was not just the responsibility of the health sector.

AGENDA 21

In June 1992, the United Nations Conference on Environment and Development (Earth Summit) was held in Rio de Janeiro, Brazil. Agenda 21 *(26)* is the United Nations programme of action for sustainable development adopted by 178 governments at the Earth Summit.

The Earth Summit brought the idea of sustainable development to the forefront of international policy and practice, and subsequently at the national and local levels. A widely used definition of the concept is: "development that meets the needs of the present, without compromising the ability of future generations to meet their own needs" *(27)*. Essentially, sustainable development is taking care of the human habitat and ensuring the protection and care of the environment, both for its own sake, and for human survival, as the health and wellbeing of present and future populations depend on the environment. Central tenets of sustainable development are therefore quality of life, equity within and between generations and social justice. Action oriented around Agenda 21 focuses on the areas that influence these factors; economic, environmental, social, political, cultural, ethical and health factors need to be addressed in an integrated way.

Agenda 21 contains more than 200 references to health, and Chapter 6 is dedicated to "protecting and promoting human health". In addition, the Rio Declaration on Environment and Health states as its first principle *(28)*: "Human beings are at the centre of concern for sustainable development. They are entitled to a healthy and productive life in harmony with nature".

Action at the local level is of key importance for the successful implementation of the ideas contained within Agenda 21, and thus for sustainable development. This is recognized in Chapter 28 of the strategy, which states that action at the local level will be a determining factor in achieving the goals of the Earth Summit. Since 1992, Local Agenda 21 initiatives to achieve sustainable development throughout the world have sought to address key issues by changing policy and practice at the local level. Successful Local Agenda 21 initiatives depend on a transition to integrated decision-making with the active participation of local communities.

The European Sustainable Cities & Towns Campaign, launched at the First European Conference on Sustainable Cities & Towns in Aalborg, Denmark in 1994, aims to reach out to local authorities to support the development of Local Agenda 21 processes throughout Europe. The core strategic tool of the campaign is a partnership of five networks of local authorities working together to promote sustainable development. One of these is the WHO Healthy Cities project.

LINKS BETWEEN HEALTH AND SUSTAINABLE DEVELOPMENT

Health and sustainable development are intimately interconnected, and lack of development adversely affects the health of many people. Nevertheless, development can harm the social and physical environment, which in turn can negatively affect health. The links between the two areas are emphasized in Fig. 2.1.

HEALTH21 has its roots within the health sector and therefore begins from a perspective of human health. It perceives sustainable development as a mechanism to improve the health, wellbeing and quality of life of human beings. Concern for the environment, economy and social issues is born out of this "human" agenda. Agenda 21 has evolved from a concern regarding the mutual relationship between development and the environment; each can affect the other positively or negatively. The consequences for human health are a primary concern. Health is therefore one of several driving forces behind Agenda 21. Perhaps the most important difference between the concept of health and that of sustainable development is one of perception. Many people wrongly perceive sustainable development as being only about environmental issues and about their global implications. As a consequence, they find it difficult to identify with the terms used and to relate the concept to practical implications. Health, in contrast, is something everyone understands intuitively and with which everyone can identify; it is an inherently human concept.

Fig. 2.1.   Conceptual model of sustainable development

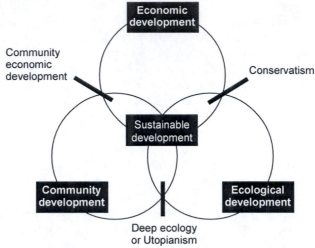

Source: Price & Dubé *(29)*

The origins of HEALTH21 and Agenda 21 are different, but they are clearly complementary, and the underlying principles and actions have many points of overlap. Table 2.1 compares the principles and processes of these two programmes. The links between health and sustainable development are discussed further in two documents produced by the WHO Healthy Cities project as part of its work with the European Sustainable Cities & Towns Campaign *(29,30)*.

Table 2.1.   Comparison between HEALTH21 and Agenda 21 principles and processes

	HEALTH21	Agenda 21
Principles		
Equity	Yes	Yes
Sustainability	Yes	Yes
Health promotion	Yes	(Health)
Intersectoral action	Yes	Yes
Community involvement	Yes	Yes
Supportive environments	Yes	Yes
International action	Yes	Yes
Processes		
Consider existing planning frameworks	Yes	Yes
Analysis of health, environment and social conditions	Yes	Yes
Public consultation on priorities	Yes	Yes
Structures for intersectoral involvement	Yes	Implicit
Vision	Yes	Yes
Long-term action plan with targets	Yes	Yes
Monitoring and evaluation	Yes	Yes

Source: adapted from Price & Dubé *(29)*

WHO HEALTHY CITIES PROJECT

Origins and evolution

The WHO Healthy Cities project was established in 1986. Its purpose was to provide a local basis for implementing the principles of the WHO strategy for health for all and the Ottawa Charter for Health Promotion. It has since evolved into a Europe-wide movement with a comprehensive mechanism for implementing health and sustainable development at the local level. HEALTH21 and Agenda 21 are its central tenets.

Hancock & Duhl *(31)* formulated the first working definition of a healthy city.

> A Healthy City is one that is continually creating and improving those physical and social environments and expanding those community resources which enable people to mutually support each other in performing all the functions of life and in developing to their maximum potential.

During the first phase of the WHO Healthy Cities project (1987–1992), this early definition was complemented by the following definition *(32)*.

> A healthy city is defined by a process and not just an outcome. A healthy city is not one that has achieved a particular health status level; it is conscious of health and striving to improve it. Thus any city can be a healthy city, regardless of its current health status; what is required is a commitment to health and a structure and process to achieve it.

In order to emphasize that these are not limiting or contradictory to other sectoral definitions, but actually encompass these, Box 2.1 indicates the main considerations that led to the formulation of the first definition. It also illustrates how different professions might view a healthy city *(31)*.

Box 2.1.   What is a healthy city?

Each person understands the concept of a healthy city differently, according to his or her own interests and training, culture and values.

   To an economist, a healthy city might be one that replaces imports in a positive frenzy of creativity and innovation; to an urban planner, a healthy city may be one that has good physical characteristics in such areas as housing, transport and green spaces; to a sociologist, a healthy city may be one that promotes social cohesion; to an educator it may be one that enables people to grow and develop; for an epidemiologist a healthy city may be one with high health status; for a health care planner it may have high-quality accessible health care services; and for average people, a healthy city may be one that enables them to make a living, keep a roof over their heads and food in their stomachs, provide for their families, meet their friends, move around safely and, in general, to freely carry out all the functions of life.

The concept of a healthy city is very broad, incorporating ideas from sociology, urban geography, urban planning, ecology, politics, economics, philosophy and a host of other disciplines in addition to public health. A healthy city means different things to different people from different cultures, from different cities and even from different districts within the same city. Thus, the health of a city cannot be described by tables of data and stacks of computer printouts alone. It must be experienced, and the assessment of the health of a city must develop and incorporate a variety of unconventional, intuitive and holistic measures to supplement hard data. Indeed, unless data are turned into stories that can be understood by everyone, they are not effective in any process of change, either political or administrative.

Box 2.2 identifies the qualities of a healthy city. The first nine points are clearly compatible with the values and responsibilities of urban planning and related professions. The last two are compatible with the values of urban planning and related professions but are not their main responsibility.

The Healthy Cities project has evolved in three distinct phases. In each phase, WHO has designated a number of cities to be members of the WHO European network (Annex 2). This is based on their ability to meet certain requirements in the way they view health and in the way they respond to the challenge of health for all. The structure of the project offers cities the space, time and legitimacy to test the process of transformation into a healthy city.

The first phase (1987–1992) involved 35 project cities and focused on the dissemination of innovative concepts relevant to health in cities, the creation of new organizational structures that act as agents for change (supported by strong political commitment) and the introduction of new methods of working for health in cities: collaboration between organizations, departments and communities.

The second phase (1993–1997) involved 38 cities, 13 of which were new in relation to the first phase. This phase was mainly directed towards action for public health policy and towards drawing up comprehensive city health plans with specific targets covering such matters as equity and sustainable development.

The third phase (1998–2002) included 41 cities (12 of which are new) as of May 2000 and was set to expand further. It is oriented towards the international policy developments of HEALTH21 and Agenda 21, building on previous experience to promote innovative and sustainable action for health in cities. The key challenge for cities in this phase is to make the transition from health promotion, which brings on board new sectors, to real intersectoral health development. Specific

Box 2.2.   The qualities of a healthy city

1.   A clean, safe physical environment of high quality (including housing quality)
2.   An ecosystem that is stable now and sustainable in the long term
3.   A strong, mutually supportive and non-exploitative community
4.   A high degree of participation and control by the public over the decisions affecting their lives, health and wellbeing
5.   The meeting of basic needs (for food, water, shelter, income, safety and work) for all the city's people
6.   Access to a wide variety of experiences and resources, with the chance for a wide variety of contact, interaction and communication
7.   A diverse, vital and innovative city economy
8.   The encouragement of connectedness with the past, with the cultural and biological heritage of city dwellers and with other groups and individuals
9.   A form that is compatible with and enhances the preceding characteristics
10.   An optimum level of appropriate public health and sick care services accessible to all
11.   High health status (high levels of positive health and low levels of disease)

Source: Hancock & Duhl (31)

priorities include preparing tools and guidance for policy development, health development planning, evaluation and monitoring. Theme areas include equity and social exclusion, sustainable development, social determinants of health, indicators, healthy settings, tobacco control and healthy urban planning. Cities taking part in the third phase work towards a set of goals that have been developed to guide the transition to a healthy city (33). A specific goal relates to urban planning (Box 2.3).

In June 1998, the International Healthy Cities Conference in Athens, Greece, marked a decade of Healthy Cities action. The event illustrated the extent to which Healthy Cities has become a significant European and global movement for change, both in the way health is viewed and in the way urban problems are addressed. The Athens Declaration for Healthy Cities (34), which reinforces the commitment of cities to the principles and processes of Healthy Cities and Local Agenda 21, has been signed by 125 city representatives.

Box 2.3.   Requirement for urban planning for cities participating in the
WHO European Healthy Cities network

Cities should carry out a programme of action to promote healthy and
sustainable urban planning policies and practice within the city.

Explanation
Urban problems are complex because of the interrelated nature of the
components of cities. Urban planning is by definition designed to regulate
the use of land in the public interest and is an important means of cities and
towns addressing sustainability issues. Planning practices and processes
need to be adapted to reflect a new awareness and to integrate health,
environmental, economic and social concerns in the twenty-first century.

Evidence for designation application
For healthy and sustainable urban planning policies and practices, cities
need to give a commitment to work in partnership with urban planners and
to outline the ways in which they intend to develop the partnership in this area.

Action required during phase III
Cities are required to review current practice and develop action for healthy
and sustainable urban planning policies and practices.

Principles
The Healthy Cities approach is based on certain key principles derived from
HEALTH21 and Local Agenda 21, and these have numerous implications for urban
planning.

Equity
Equity in health means that everyone has the right and the opportunity to realize
their full potential *(32)*. The political, economic and social inequality of groups of
citizens clearly influences their state of health.

European cities show visible signs of many aspects of inequality. Social
segregation is common, combined with the degradation of living space, both in
housing and the urban fabric. Many people living in urban areas have limited or no
access to leisure, cultural, commercial and administrative services, good safe
meeting places, clean air and efficient public transport. *The solid facts: the social
determinants of health (16)* describes the effects on health of people's social and
economic circumstances, examining issues such as unemployment, social exclusion
and transport.

Fig. 2.2.   Addressing inequalities in health: links for action

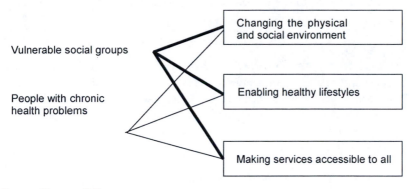

Source: Tsouros *(32)*

Equity policies involve improving the living and working standards of disadvantaged people and raising the standards of physical and social environments. Urban planning has an important opportunity and a responsibility to reduce inequality in health; this is illustrated within the wider context in Fig. 2.2. Making equity central to the urban planning process means bearing in mind the needs of different social groups, generations and genders.

Sustainability

The Athens Declaration for Healthy Cities *(34)* says that "Densely populated cities and urban regions provide vital settings for the implementation of important policies that combine environmental, economic, social and health objectives.". The principle of sustainability lies at the very heart of the Healthy Cities approach; the health and wellbeing of a city's people is an important indicator of the success of policies for sustainable development.

Many urban planners are becoming involved in Local Agenda 21 initiatives, and many more are considering issues of sustainable development in their day-to-day working practices. Given that the well established role of urban planning is to regulate the use and quality of the urban environment in the interests of the public, the need to manage and develop cities in a sustainable fashion should be a key principle of any urban planning initiative. However, most urban planning systems in Europe do not address issues of sustainability effectively. Some respond primarily to powerful economic interests (especially in the western part of the European Region), and many interpret sustainability only in terms of a narrow role in environmental protection. The Healthy Cities approach provides urban planners with an opportunity to ensure that their practices become more sustainable, both in the decisions made and in the decision-making process. It also underlines the importance of health and quality of life: human beings should be at the centre of the desire for sustainability.

Towards a new planning process – a guide to reorienting urban planning towards Local Agenda 21 (8) explores the issue of sustainability in urban planning in more detail.

Intersectoral cooperation

The Athens Declaration for Healthy Cities *(34)* says that "Health is promoted most effectively when agencies from many sectors work together and learn from each other.". Since health is created or damaged in the living environment, it is influenced by the actions and decisions of the majority of municipal administrative sectors as well as by those of the private sector. The sectors involved can be defined both in terms of organization and topic and include:

- health, social, environmental and economic;
- public, private, voluntary and academic;
- levels of government – national, regional, local and community; and
- agencies engaged in serving the public and providing infrastructure.

The traditional approach to addressing urban issues is based on the development in the nineteenth century of strong and separate disciplines. Hancock *(35)* describes this approach and points out that most of the problems faced in the twenty-first century cut across these boundaries. Fig. 2.3 summarizes these ideas.

Intersectoral cooperation allows duplication and confusion to be kept to a minimum while optimizing the use of resources and results, achieving maximum synergy and efficiency. Cooperation between urban planners and other sectors of local government, as well as the private sector, is required to address today's urban problems effectively. A new directive from the European Commission on strategic environmental assessment of land-use plans and the way they are produced will

Fig. 2.3.   Twenty-first-century problems and nineteenth-century structures

	Public works	Parks	Traffic	Public health	Planning	Environmental health	
Healthy city							Twenty-first-century problems
Sustainability							
Equity							
Mobility							
Energy							
Food							

Nineteenth-century structures

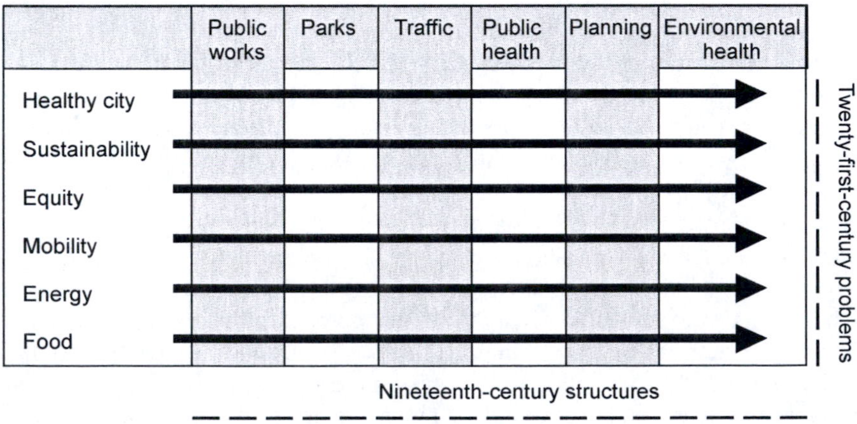

Source: WHO Regional Office for Europe *(30)*

have significant implications for collaboration between agencies in the European Union countries and will require greater integration of health objectives into both strategic environmental assessment and environmental impact assessment.

Intersectoral cooperation can be extremely difficult to achieve. Individuals, including civil servants, professionals and politicians, may resist, motivated both by their sectoral view of problems and by worry about losing their identity and/or professional privileges. Another cause is the perceived lack of effective ways to manage the change needed in working practices. In terms of intersectoral cooperation, the value of the Healthy Cities approach lies in its ability to stimulate and guide such changes in working practices.

Chapter 4 discusses the process of developing intersectoral cooperation in the strategic planning process to promote health in cities.

Community involvement

Informed, motivated and actively participating communities are key partners in setting priorities and making and implementing decisions *(36)*. The oldest recognition of the role and responsibility of the citizen in the development of a city is clearly expressed in the oath a foreigner had to take on acquiring Athenian citizenship in ancient Greece: "we shall leave this city bigger, better and more beautiful than it was left to us" *(37)*.

HEALTH21 *(24)* underlines the need for community participation in decisions affecting human health. Promoting health also means contributing to the development of the community: community development aims to make individuals and communities able to grow and change their needs and priorities *(25)*. This means encouraging people to define their needs and to seek their own solutions. *Community participation in local health and sustainable development: a working document on approaches and techniques (38)* explores community involvement in more detail.

In urban planning, the right to participation derives from the citizen's right to be informed and consulted in the decision-making processes affecting the area in which he or she lives. Different levels of participation are appropriate for different stages of the urban planning process (Fig. 2.4) *(39)*.

In practice, community participation in the urban planning process is limited throughout Europe. Planning systems in some countries do not acknowledge the need for such a process, maintaining that the public officials know what is best for the public good. Others may have processes for consulting citizens, but these do not really constitute full participation in the decision-making process. In some instances the process is manipulated to achieve a certain result; in other cases a consultation process is used merely to legitimize decisions already taken. Sometimes political, technical and administrative authorities allow citizens to comment only on plans that have already been prepared, implying that the authorities do not necessarily have to take these comments on board. Comments made in this way at a late stage in the planning process cannot take into account all the relevant issues and will almost certainly be very generic.

Fig. 2.4.   The wheel of participation

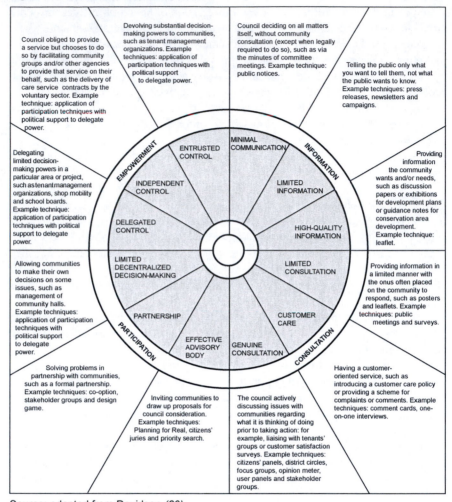

Council obliged to provide a service but chooses to do so by facilitating community groups and/or other agencies to provide that service on their behalf, such as the delivery of care service contracts by the voluntary sector. Example technique: application of participation techniques with political support to delegate power.

Devolving substantial decision-making powers to communities, such as tenant management organizations. Example techniques: application of participation techniques with political support to delegate power.

Council deciding on all matters itself, without community consultation (except when legally required to do so), such as via the minutes of committee meetings. Example technique: public notices.

Telling the public only what you want to tell them, not what the public wants to know. Example techniques: press releases, newsletters and campaigns.

Delegating limited decision-making powers in a particular area or project, such as tenant management organizations, shop mobility and school boards. Example technique: application of participation techniques with political support to delegate power.

Providing information the community wants and/or needs, such as discussion papers or exhibitions for development plans or guidance notes for conservation area development. Example technique: leaflet.

Allowing communities to make their own decisions on some issues, such as management of community halls. Example techniques: application of participation techniques with political support to delegate power.

Providing information in a limited manner with the onus often placed on the community to respond, such as posters and leaflets. Example techniques: public meetings and surveys.

Solving problems in partnership with communities, such as a formal partnership. Example techniques: co-option, stakeholder groups and design game.

Inviting communities to draw up proposals for council consideration. Example techniques: Planning for Real, citizens' juries and priority search.

The council actively discussing issues with communities regarding what it is thinking of doing prior to taking action: for example, liaising with tenants' groups or customer satisfaction surveys. Example techniques: citizens' panels, district circles, focus groups, opinion meter, user panels and stakeholder groups.

Having a customer-oriented service, such as introducing a customer care policy or providing a scheme for complaints or comments. Example techniques: comment cards, one-on-one interviews.

EMPOWERMENT — ENTRUSTED CONTROL, INDEPENDENT CONTROL, DELEGATED CONTROL, LIMITED DECENTRALIZED DECISION-MAKING, PARTNERSHIP, EFFECTIVE ADVISORY BODY — PARTICIPATION

MINIMAL COMMUNICATION, LIMITED INFORMATION, HIGH-QUALITY INFORMATION — INFORMATION

LIMITED CONSULTATION, CUSTOMER CARE, GENUINE CONSULTATION — CONSULTATION

Source: adapted from Davidson *(39)*

As Richard Rogers highlights *(37)*, the community can be involved in the decision-making process by using the built environment as a teaching tool: cities are an excellent living laboratory. Encouraging examples can be found all over the world, showing that suitably managed public participation in urban planning, architecture and ecology can transform the physical and social layout of the city. New techniques, such as Planning for Real *(38)*, community architecture *(40)* and the charrette process (Chapter 5) are examples. These initiatives underline the need for urban planners and architects to learn the techniques of mediation and leadership so as to carry out their projects in close collaboration with the end-users (citizens).

Box 2.4.   The inhabitants participate in drawing up a master
plan in Segovia (Spain)

Segovia is a town with 60 000 inhabitants in the heart of the Castile-León region and is included in the UNESCO World Heritage List. Its master plan was drawn up in collaboration with its inhabitants, whose needs and wishes were taken into consideration. Various groups of interest were identified, each one of which was provided with a questionnaire that listed the salient points of the plan. During the meetings with the local authorities, each group sketched out the functions and services it considered indispensable. The various suggestions were then reported in a summary that indicated the points of agreement and disagreement. The planners used the summary to identify the aims and essential requirements of the plan and to decide their order of priority. Finally, in a meeting with all the groups, the results of the exercise were compared and the final decisions received general approval. Among the 50 plans currently being realized in Spain's provincial capitals, the Segovia plan is the only one to have received unanimous approval. On this basis, the authorities can count on the real support of the residents and on their active involvement in the life of the town.

Source: WHO Regional Office for Europe *(6)*

International action and solidarity

The Healthy Cities project is based on the spirit of real cooperation, not only among municipal sectors, but also between cities and countries; national and international networks have been established to promote the exchange of resources, knowledge, information and experience, offering mutual support and developing new strategies. This eases communication problems resulting from differences in language and working practices.

Urban planning systems and practices vary widely across Europe, and opportunities for urban planners to learn from and experience each other's ways of working are limited. Nevertheless, the same urban problems are evident in many European countries, and in western Europe, legislation and policy developments from the European Commission influence planning thought and procedure. The Healthy Cities movement provides an excellent opportunity for urban planners across Europe to learn from each other, sharing experience about how to create more healthy, sustainable and people-oriented urban environments.

Working towards healthy cities

The WHO Healthy Cities Project Office provides support to the cities that are part of the WHO European network by coordinating, monitoring and evaluating their activities. It also organizes a series of meetings on the operational aspects of working towards healthy cities and on specific themes such as smoking, alcohol, transport and health and healthy urban planning.

As the Healthy Cities project has evolved, in collaboration with universities and experts from all over the world, WHO has produced a series of documents and databases regarding the theoretical and practical aspects of the project *(38,41)*. These describe in detail the strategic and operational mechanisms of the project, document the experiences of cities in the WHO European network and assess the results obtained to date. Many of these documents can be downloaded from the Healthy Cities Web site at http://www.who.dk/healthy-cities.

The principles discussed above provide the background for the work of the Healthy Cities project. In terms of activity, the approach comprises four key operational elements that together provide a basis for the transition to a healthy city, as shown below.

The Healthy Cities approach – four ways of working	
A Explicit political commitment at the highest level to the principles and strategies of the Healthy Cities project	B Establishment of new organizational structures to manage change
C Commitment to developing a shared vision for the city, with a health plan and work on specific themes	D Investment in formal and informal networking and cooperation

The development of healthy urban planning practices can be supported through these four elements.

A – Political commitment

Reorienting urban decision-making processes towards health and sustainable development requires changing how decisions are made and how different sectors implement these decisions. This can only be achieved with political support at the highest level, since change needs to disseminate throughout the whole city and not just in one department or area of work. It requires political endorsement of the principles and strategies of health for all, Agenda 21, the Ottawa Charter for Health Promotion and the Healthy Cities project.

Cities designated to work within the WHO European network have made an official commitment, through the mayor and the representatives of different sectors on behalf of the whole city council, to the principles and methods of health for all and the Healthy Cities project. Support for this process across political parties is important. The political stability of the local government affects the success of the local project, and the most successful project cities are those in which all parties have developed a consensus on the importance of health and sustainable development. Health should not be a partisan political issue – it is everybody's business.

B – Organizational structures

The principle of intersectoral cooperation and its importance in achieving healthy and sustainable cities was explored previously. The WHO Healthy Cities project helps cities to manage the change in working methods, supporting the development of such cooperation. Cities taking part in the third phase of the project must have established an intersectoral steering group that oversees the strategy and work of the project. A project coordinator is also appointed. The exact structures vary between cities, and many are beginning to develop additional intersectoral working

Fig. 2.5.   City of Belfast Healthy City Project

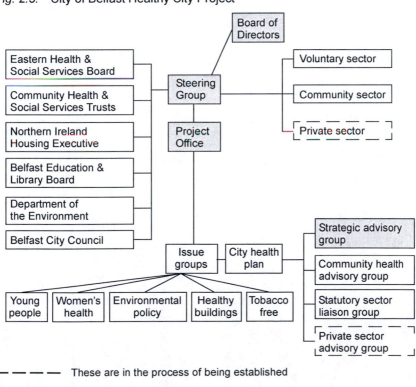

— — — —   These are in the process of being established

[ ]   Decision-making groups

Source: Belfast Healthy Cities *(42)*

groups to address work around particular themes.

The establishment of these structures also includes the development of city-wide partnerships for health. The need for intersectoral cooperation should extend beyond the boundaries of the city administration to include representatives of local businesses, community groups and nongovernmental organizations, and these should be represented within the organization of the project. Fig. 2.5 illustrates the organizational structure of the Belfast Healthy City Project. Fig. 2.6 illustrates examples of how the different steering groups in a city might be organized.

C – Realizing a shared vision

The shared vision for the health of a city is expressed in a health plan. The nature of such plans has evolved with the project, to reflect the strengthening of partnerships for health in cities. Cities produced city health plans in the second phase of the WHO Healthy Cities project. In the third phase, cities are working to integrate health objectives more effectively within city structures to produce the city health development plan.

Fig. 2.6.   Members of a healthy city project steering group

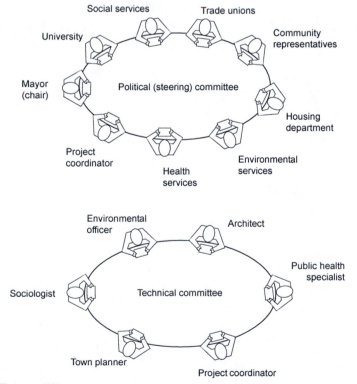

Source: Tsouros *(32)*

The process

The development of a vision for the health of the city is as much about the process, and what the city learns about itself from that process, as it is about a product; a city health development plan that addresses how the different sectors and actors within the city will work towards improving people's health and quality of life. Work on addressing health through specific themes such as transport, tobacco, caring for vulnerable groups or healthy urban planning is an integral part of this process and should be reflected in the city health development plan.

City planning for health and sustainable development (30) states:

> A city health plan is much more than a fixed description or inventory of problems, resources and solutions. It is an opportunity to re-discover the fact that many people have a role to play in making cities healthier and more sustainable and that planning should be a dynamic process involving many partners.

The importance of intersectoral cooperation in creating the conditions for success for the plan, both in terms of content and the likelihood of implementation, is outlined in *City health planning – the framework (36)*. Each city is free to appoint the people in charge of drawing up the plan, but the following categories should be included *(36)*:

- politicians and planners in the highest hierarchical positions, in order to ensure political acceptance and implementation of the plan;
- representatives of the various public sectors that influence the state of health, in particular: environment, education, urban planning and building, transport, employment, social services and health care;
- voluntary organizations and special interest groups;
- categories of health care professionals, including general practitioners and hospitals;
- other groups of specialists that are to contribute to developing the strategies and policies for implementing the plan's proposals; and
- community participation in each stage of preparation.

Fig. 2.7 illustrates how politicians, professionals and the community all perform an important role in the process of planning city health development.

Three main operational tools are used in this process:

- the health information system
- the health profile
- the city health development plan.

Fig. 2.7.   The pillars of health

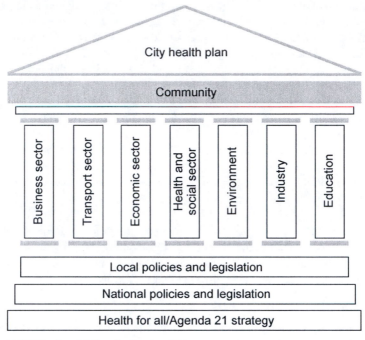

Source: WHO Regional Office for Europe *(30)*

The health information system

The Healthy Cities project uses a number of indicators to identify the initial actions in each city and, subsequently, to measure progress through continual monitoring and updating (Annex 3). The majority of these are not found in health literature but are extremely pertinent as they reflect the quality of life of city inhabitants. Many of the indicators are relevant to urban planning and may also be collected for environmental or sustainability information bases within cities. Each city integrates this list with other indicators, according to local needs and characteristics, and they form the basic health information system. Cities use this information, which is collected on a regular basis, to draw up a city health profile.

The health profile

A city health profile is a public health report that brings together key pieces of information on health and its determinants in the city and interprets and analyses the information. The profile identifies in writing and graphics health problems and their potential solutions in a specific city *(43,44)*. The profile is aimed at identifying the priority and secondary areas for action and forms the information basis for the preparation of a city health plan.

This tool is not an end in itself, but part of a dynamic process. Profiles should be produced on a regular basis. This enables "targets for progress to be set, the implementation of recommendations to be monitored, and achievements measured, recorded and celebrated" *(43)*.

The city health development plan

Using information from indicators and the city health profile, each city has drawn up an action plan called a city health plan. This highlights future areas of work and chosen priorities.

The city health plans set out strategies and programmes of intervention to improve health in the city, define targets and timetables for achieving proposed actions and identify monitoring arrangements *(43)*.

City health plans are not health care plans but part of a process to develop a common vision of healthy and sustainable communities, as well as a tangible tool for their implementation. In the third phase of the WHO Healthy Cities project, the city health plan has been replaced by the city health development plan. This is similar to previous health plans in the issues it addresses but requires stronger collaboration with other sectors than previously and a focus on developing health rather than promoting health.

In the past, health plans were essentially health promotion plans, the most successful of which identified activities that should be carried out in other sectors to promote health. In the third phase, health planning focuses more on such issues as sustainability, equity and social development, and in this way mobilizes a much wider range of partners for health. City health development planning also strengthens strategic partnerships in cities to produce an integrated strategy for health development. This strategy is then implemented through the activities of different sectors, and the role of each sector is therefore reflected in the plan. In this way, the process of planning city health development strengthens the role each sector plays in working for health, wellbeing and the quality of life in the city.

Urban planners have an important role to play in producing and implementing the city health development plan. The need for supportive environments in developing healthy city initiatives is recognized as one of the key principles of city health development planning *(36)*: "The creation of supportive physical and social environments should be addressed in the plan. This includes issues of ecology and sustainability as well as aspects such as social networks, transport, housing and other environmental concerns.". Boxes 2.5 and 2.6 provide case studies of health plans and draw out issues of relevance to urban planning.

City health development plans are also of use to urban planners in that they can provide supplementary information on the city in general and specifically on subjects regarding health. This includes an indication of the parts of the city in which the greatest health problems are concentrated; areas that should be first on the list for further analysis to identify any opportunities where urban planning initiatives can improve the situation.

Box 2.5.   City health planning in Copenhagen (Denmark)

The City of Copenhagen developed one of the earliest city health plans *(45)*. It had specific targets and actions to be implemented in the period 1994– 1997 (Fig. 2.8).

  The subjects related to urban planning are identification of local areas, intersectoral cooperation, community participation, equity, housing, transport, public spaces and monitoring and evaluation.

Identification of local areas. The city health plan is based on the assumption that health promotion should be carried out at the smallest appropriate geographical level. The Copenhagen city plan (master plan) identifies 15 administrative districts as local areas in the city. Work is envisaged to determine whether the boundaries of theses districts coincide with the boundaries of "local areas" as perceived by the citizens or whether smaller residential areas or neighbourhoods are more appropriate.

Intersectoral cooperation. The plan not only emphasizes the importance of intersectoral cooperation, but gives a series of conceptual explanations.

•   The need for coordination among specialists reflects the recognition that there are numerous areas of contact between different disciplines.
•   Communication and dialogue between sectors rather than de-specialization is the key to effective intersectoral cooperation. Professionals must be trained to develop their ability to listen to and understand other groups of specialists.
•   Individuals get inspired by knowing that the participation of one's own sector is necessary for effective cooperation.

Community participation. The plan proposes that community participation work be developed so that citizens can be adequately informed, oriented and motivated to participate with awareness in the various initiatives.

Equity. The aim to reduce inequality among the various urban areas is a priority.

Housing. Citizens' proposals to renew some of the more deteriorated districts were analysed. The intention is to reverse the tendency to "expel" those who currently reside in an area after it has been renewed. Particular attention

Fig. 2.8   Framework of the city health plan of Copenhagen

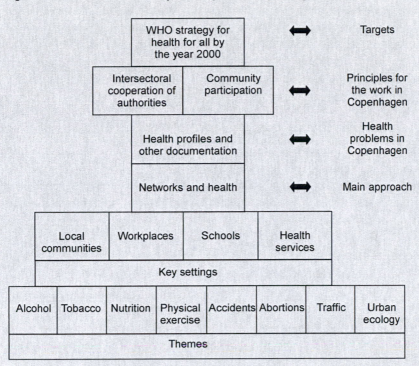

Source: Healthy City Project, Copenhagen Health Services *(45)*, p. 77

is paid to families with children. The plan proposes building small blocks of flats with dimensions suitable for various sizes of family and a maintenance programme aimed at keeping an acceptable standard of quality over time. With regard to the technical aspects of renewal in so-called grey urban renewal areas (usually peripheral neighbourhoods developed in the 1930s), projects targeting the quality and size of the dwellings combined with simultaneous upgrading of surrounding areas (recreational facilities, services and other amenities) are proposed. A project to renew the Mønten residential complex and another complex in the Skoleholder area (both in the Bispebjerg district) is in progress; this is set up within the framework of a neighbourhood plan and the active participation of tenants and owners.

Transport. Compared with other European cities of similar size, Copenhagen stands out for its efficient public transport, flow of traffic and predominance of bicycle paths. The health plan cites initiatives aimed at reducing road accidents involving bicyclists and protecting the most exposed residential areas from noise and atmospheric pollution. Work predicted during the plan period included: reconstructing some roads, studying measures to make it feasible to cover distances exceeding 5–10 km by bicycle, building a further 12 km of bicycle paths, implementing structural measures to increase the safety of bicycle paths and controlling heavy vehicle circulation on the narrowest roads in the city.

Public spaces. Improving green spaces and creating a network of linked green spaces throughout the urban area were identified as a priority. In addition, the plan sought to transform some local streets into recreational areas (some initiatives have already been implemented in the Nørrebro area) and to create public spaces for social life (two squares have been enlarged in the Vesterbro area).

Monitoring and evaluation. The results achieved by implementing the plan are to be assessed by monitoring the changes (indicators) and the processes of community participation and intersectoral cooperation.

Box 2.6.   City health development planning in Stoke on Trent (United Kingdom)

Background. The City of Stoke on Trent was designated as a participant in the WHO European Healthy Cities network in 1998. Work began on preparing the city health development plan in summer 1998. The City Council launched *Sharpening the focus on health: a city health development plan* in November 1999.

Process. The City established a core working group responsible for developing the document. This debated the scope of the plan and its relationship to other planning instruments in the city. The group concluded that it should be a key document integrating all the work in the city influencing health. The vision, strategy and priorities for action outlined in the plan were developed after the city's key health priorities had been identified through a series of health-profiling exercises. The different sectors whose activities contribute to the development of health in the city were then asked to identify what they were doing in relation to the priorities and to develop part of the plan.

This process ensured that public health specialists in Stoke on Trent and the City Council were formally linked, and this prompted their input into council strategies such as a local transport plan and the development of an Assistant Director's Health Agenda Group. This is an interdepartmental group set up to develop a corporate perspective on health issues and feed information into the political arena. Urban planners play an important role in this group.

Health indicators are now being developed as part of the City's urban renewal and regeneration initiatives. In addition, the Healthy City Project coordinator acts as an enabler to develop tools such as health impact assessment, ensuring that health is considered within priority areas such as housing, environment, transport, economic development and urban planning.

Content. The vision for improving health in Stoke on Trent centres around active community participation in decision-making processes, promoting equity and intersectoral collaboration to improve health and the quality of life. Priorities for action centre on issues of lifestyle, economic development, education, poverty, environment, crime, transport, housing and access to health care. For each of these issues, the plan elaborates on conditions in the city, how these will be tackled, links to relevant local plans and programmes and what specific action will be taken. Links to the city plan (or urban land-use plan) are made in a number of areas, and action that falls either wholly or partly within the remit of urban planners are identified. The examples of housing and transport are examined below.

Housing. The city health development plan identifies problems such as poor-quality private-sector housing, aging public-sector housing, inability of people to pay for heating, a significant number of elderly people in unsuitable accommodation, community safety issues and some poor housing environments. Strategies to address these problems are outlined, with links made to the city plan (the urban plan), the corporate plan and a number of initiatives related to regeneration, housing, community development and equity. Specific types of action are outlined. They include:

- meeting housing need and aspirations by developing affordable accommodation through effective planning, commissioning and good design;
- developing options to relieve the problem of properties in the private and public sectors that are in low demand;
- creating and maintaining balanced communities by tackling social exclusion and poverty and encouraging housing choice and mobility;

- dealing with unfit housing through renovation or clearance options as identified in stock condition surveys;
- developing specialist housing projects where needed; and
- extending partnerships with residents' associations and organizations assisting with community development and advice.

Transport. The plan discusses the positive and negative aspects of transport choices on health and identifies a variety of strategies to tackle negative aspects and to promote healthy transport options. These strategies include commuter planning, walking, cycling and public transport, and links are made to the city plan (urban land-use plan), Local Agenda 21 activities, and environmental, health and regeneration strategies in the city. A wide range of activities are proposed to take forward these strategies. Those of particular relevance to urban planners are including health in transport strategies and promoting more cycling and walking.

Health will be included in transport strategies by such means as the following.

- A local transport plan will be developed by July 2000 for the period 2001–2006. This will improve the urban environment through initiatives to reduce congestion and improve traffic management, with particular emphasis on sustainable development patterns. Improving people's health is one of the aims of the strategy.
- A new city plan will be produced and published in 2002. It will set out guidelines to increase mobility and accessibility for all residents of Stoke on Trent, with particular attention given to non-car owners and disabled people.
- A green travel plan for the City Council will be produced by April 2000 that will advocate progressive policies to alternative transport modes.

Cycling and walking will be promoted by such means as:

- preparing an implementation plan for the city's cycling strategy to increase the number of people using bicycles, and to ensure that long-term facilities are considered for cyclists;
- implementing the national cycle network through the city;
- extending cycle routes to respond to identified needs for commuter journeys, routes to shops and leisure facilities in addition to safe routes to school;

- producing maps of cycle routes and current facilities for cyclists across the city, including information on the health benefits;
- ensuring that new developments give consideration to pedestrians and cyclists;
- ensuring that pedestrians' and cyclists' needs are considered in various forums, committees and groups; and
- encouraging and facilitating the development of walking and cycling routes for leisure purposes.

Conclusions. The process of producing the city health development plan was extremely important in allowing people from a number of sectors to think about health as it relates to their work. It illustrated how the work of each different sector contributed to realizing the vision of improving health, wellbeing and the quality of life in Stoke on Trent. Urban planners played a vital role in this process, not only in terms of work on the health profile and developing an overall picture of the City's needs but also in developing plans for the future to meet those needs.

Source: Stoke on Trent Healthy City *(46)*

D – Networking
National and international networks
In addition to cities in the WHO European network, the Healthy Cities movement includes national and thematic networks. Over 1000 cities and towns are linked to Healthy Cities networks in 29 European countries (Fig. 2.9) *(47)*.

Since WHO cannot support all healthy city projects directly, national Healthy Cities networks have been developed for cities with the same language and institutional and regulatory framework. WHO liaises with the coordinators of the national networks. Their activities include translating the strategy and guidance documents of the project into national languages, producing newsletters, publicizing the Healthy Cities movement on a national basis and organizing meetings and workshops to discuss strategic issues or particular topics.

Thematic networks known as multi-city action plans exist at the national and international levels to work on specific topic areas *(48)*. Each multi-city action plan defines its own objectives, but the broad targets of all multi-city action plans are:

Fig. 2.9.   Countries in the WHO European Region with healthy cities

- combined action aimed at developing and completing programmes, policies, documents and innovative declarations;
- developing know-how for other cities; and
- involving other partners within cities, besides those from the healthy city project office, in international networking.

Past and current themes for multi-city action plans have included: Agenda 21, active living, tobacco, the Baltic sub-region, women, nutrition and road accidents.

A thematic network on healthy urban planning is emerging in Europe. In October 1999, urban planners, healthy city project coordinators and academics from 19 cities in the WHO Healthy Cities network across Europe met in Milan to discuss the concept of healthy urban planning (*49,50*). Debate and discussion included the meaning of healthy urban planning, what type of support and guidance urban planners and healthy city projects need to realize healthy urban planning and how the network should proceed in developing future work in this area. Much enthusiasm was expressed for the ideas presented, and many new suggestions were made as to how both cities and WHO could make progress in this area. It was recommended that WHO establish a city action group on healthy urban planning. This group would test guidance, contribute to the development of new tools and act as a support network for city initiatives. It would work in a more focused way and in closer collaboration with WHO than has been the case with multi-city action plans.

CONCLUSIONS

This chapter focuses primarily on the activities of cities that are part of the WHO Healthy Cities network and cities that are part of healthy cities networks within their own countries. Urban planners located in these cities can make a valuable contribution to the city health planning process, and the Healthy Cities approach can in turn enhance and improve urban planning policy and practice.

In summary, the Healthy Cities approach is important for urban planning for the following reasons.

• It stimulates the development of sound urban planning policy and practice, both in a general sense and more specifically in the areas of equity, sustainability and community participation.
• It provides further legitimacy for existing urban planning policy and practice that is sound or healthy.
• It facilitates intersectoral cooperation in cities. Urban planners can benefit from such cooperation, as this cooperation minimizes duplication and avoids discrepancy between the policies of different sectors. This enables policy initiatives to be more successfully implemented.
• Through networking mechanisms, the Healthy Cities approach provides an opportunity for urban planners to make contact with fellow professionals at the national and international levels. Urban planners across Europe face similar problems. Healthy Cities allows them to share experience and solutions.
• Political support for the Healthy Cities approach provides the necessary support, at the highest level locally, for the principles and policies associated with healthy urban planning.

The Healthy Cities approach is not restrictive. Urban planners who work in cities that are not part of the worldwide Healthy Cities movement may feel inspired to make changes in their working practices in accordance with the Healthy Cities principles. Urban planners can:

• begin to develop intersectoral networks and partnerships within their own cities, improving communication between different sectors of local government and with local business and communities; and
• re-examine urban planning practices so that health is a priority consideration in the decision-making process: for example, making the health and wellbeing of the citizens of the city a central objective of the urban plan or land-use plan.

Chapter 3

Healthy urban planning in practice – experiences of cities in the Healthy Cities movement

INTRODUCTION

Previous chapters underlined the links between health and urban planning, illustrating the value of the Healthy Cities approach and the importance of healthy urban planning. This chapter establishes a baseline for future work in this area. The WHO Healthy Cities project has existed since 1986 in Europe, but cities were first formally required to involve urban planners in this work in the third phase of the project (1998–2002). Healthy urban planning is a new area of work for the Healthy Cities movement, and WHO therefore carried out a survey of urban planners in the cities that are part of the WHO Healthy Cities network at the end of the second phase of the project (1993–1997) *(51)*.

This chapter explores the results of that survey. It examines the extent to which the principles promoted by cities that are part of the WHO European Healthy Cities network are already incorporated into urban planning processes and the level to which the concept of healthy urban planning has developed in cities. The survey results are complemented by comments, examples and case studies from network cities across Europe.

The survey is especially relevant to cities that are part of the Healthy Cities movement but is also of interest to urban planners throughout Europe. First, the questionnaire responses and the examples given indicate similarities and differences in the way urban planning problems are approached in different countries. Second, the survey provides evidence that healthy urban planning can indeed become a reality.

As this chapter will show, this work is in its early stages. However, the intersectoral nature of Healthy Cities work has meant that, in a number of cities across Europe, links have been made between healthy city projects and urban planners, with joint work taking place at different levels. In some instances this has taken place at the level of individual regeneration or renewal projects, and in others it has changed how the whole urban area is planned.

SURVEY OF CITIES PARTICIPATING IN THE SECOND PHASE OF THE WHO EUROPEAN NETWORK

Background
The survey of cities participating in the second phase of the WHO European Healthy Cities network was carried out to find out more about the views of urban planners on the relationship between health and urban planning and to establish whether urban planners in these cities have considered health, wellbeing and quality of life in their work. The results could then inform the emerging WHO initiative to develop the concept and practice of healthy urban planning.

Methods
In May 1998, a questionnaire was sent to the heads of all urban planning departments in cities participating in the second phase (1993–1997) of the WHO Healthy Cities project (Annex 2). The main objectives of the questionnaire were to explore:

- how the respondents interpret the relationship between health and urban planning;
- how the principles of healthy urban planning influence the practice of urban planning;
- problems concerned with setting priorities and proposing solutions;
- obstacles to realizing plans and proposals;
- the state of the art and results of the most significant strategies, policies or projects.

The questionnaire was subdivided into three sections:

- urban planning practices in each city;
- the involvement of urban planners in the local healthy city project; and
- perceptions of healthy urban planning both in theory and in practice.

Analysis of responses
The response rate was 76% (29 of 38 cities). Many of the answers were generic, and this presented a problem as they did not provide specific examples. In addition, although the first two sections contained generic questions and the third section contained specific conceptual and operational questions, answers were often duplicated and included many thematic variations.

In order to facilitate analysis of the questionnaires, the responses were rationalized. The same concepts expressed in various ways were categorized as being the same answers. At the same time, oversimplification was avoided since this would have prevented the recognition of different interpretations. The analysis was carried out bearing in mind the guiding principles and action areas of healthy urban planning.

APPLYING HEALTHY CITIES PRINCIPLES TO URBAN PLANNING

The questionnaire examined the extent to which certain key principles of the WHO Healthy Cities project (Chapter 2) – equity, intersectoral cooperation and community involvement – had been incorporated into urban planning practices.

Equity

A healthy approach to urban planning is an approach that promotes equity and social cohesion. Healthy urban planning involves planning for everyone in the city and not just responding to the most powerful or most vocal interests. The case study in Box 3.1 shows how the principle of equity can be consciously integrated into the urban planning process.

Box 3.1.   Promoting equity in Milan (Italy)

In 1990, the City of Milan began a project known as the Healthy Urban Child *(52)*. This project involved children throughout Milan in designing their own neighbourhoods, so that these neighbourhoods would be more responsive to children's needs and desires. It also sought to allow children to have a voice within the urban planning process. First, with help from teachers and experts, pupils analysed the state of their local area. They looked at urban planning, transport and traffic, places to socialize, green spaces and play areas. Next they produced designs, plans and models explaining their ideas for improvements. Five of the children's plans were selected to be realized. The professional team included architects who were experts in designing with children, urban planners, an urban anthropologist, teachers and traffic police.

The outcomes of the project included the following.

- Places used traditionally only as squares were reviewed, looking at how they could be developed to accommodate other activities.
- Roads originally conceived as routes for vehicular traffic were reclassified to allow for pedestrian and bicycle traffic and to provide places for children to play so that they would feel that they were in a more natural context.
- Green spaces already used as play or social areas were improved in terms of increasing the number of uses.
- Interior and exterior spaces in nursery schools were redesigned in order to maximize play opportunities and permit staff and children to modify the spatial arrangements depending on the need and functions.

The project also stimulated further changes in how the city is managed.

- The staff of the City were remotivated through their experiences with the project.
- Urban planners became much more aware of children's requirements in a general sense.
- The whole neighbourhood became involved in the project through the families of the schoolchildren.
- The school became used as a neighbourhood resource.
- Children, families, staff and residents developed an increased sense of belonging and caring for the neighbourhood.
- People increasingly recognized the value of cultural and environmental diversity as essential components of healthy, sustainable cities.

This example shows that the various elements of a healthy urban planning process are inherently linked. The Healthy Urban Child project began as an exercise in involving children in urban planning, but its results and influence have a much wider sphere.

The responses to the survey of urban planners in the 38 WHO European network cities on the subject of vulnerable groups illustrate how urban planners currently take the needs of all citizens into account. The cities were asked how they planned for different groups such as children or elderly people. The answers have been subdivided into three groups expressed in terms of their compatibility with the principles of healthy urban planning:

- compatible: working groups are formed with the participation of interested people;
- partly compatible: specific needs are taken into consideration but without the active participation of interested people (information analysis); and
- incompatible: when citizens are considered as an abstract and general population.

Table 3.1 contains detailed results. It indicates the types of initiatives taken. Some cities gave more than one answer, and since it was considered important to reflect all the answers in the results tables, no percentages are given. One of the 29 respondents did not respond to this question. Fig. 3.1 provides summarized results.

Table 3.1.   Results of a survey of cities (n = 29, 37 total responses) participating in the second phase of the WHO Healthy Cities project on using urban planning to promote equity and the compatibility of urban planning practice with equity considerations

Questionnaire responses by compatibility category	Number	
Compatible with the principles of healthy urban planning	**10**	
Creating work groups of planners and interested people		5
Grouping various needs for public spaces		2
Providing services close to housing		1
Producing local plans for special groups		1
Providing special facilities: such as ones for elderly people, housing and parks		1
Partly compatible with the principles of healthy urban planning	**15**	
Creating safe roads		1
Consulting social and educational services to obtain information		3
Assessing citizens' requests		1
Involving local groups on an occasional basis		2
Consulting the district council		1
Producing intersectoral plans		5
Initiating special programmes		1
Specific research		1
Incompatible with the principles of healthy urban planning	**11**	
Applying standards imposed by law		8
Using the experience of the planner		1
Creating multifunctional areas		1
These things are not generally considered		1
No response	**1**	

A selection of responses relating to urban planning and equity issues are included below. These comments illustrate a variety of approaches in considering different groups in the urban planning process.

• The development plan provides for the overall development of the city. A series of integrated action plans which focus on local areas caters for the special needs of different groups.

• Planning for the needs of the various subgroups in our city takes place in different stages of planning. When preparing the municipal work programme, a large number of target populations are defined, so that when the municipal departments determine their tasks, they must also ascertain which particular sector of the population is being served. This allows for a detailed analysis of whether each of the city's tasks meet the needs of each target population and region of the city as well as the goals and objectives set by the city; this analysis

Fig. 3.1.   Results of a survey of cities (n = 29, 37 total responses) participating in the second phase of the WHO Healthy Cities project on using urban planning to promote equity and the compatibility of urban planning practice with equity considerations

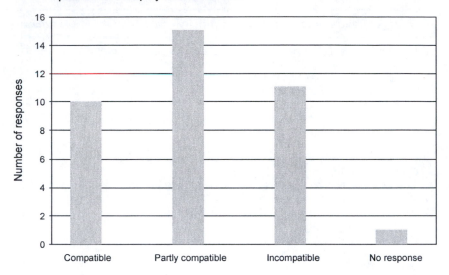

is conducted upon the completion of the 1-year and multi-year programmes by the city's departments. The municipal work programme system is also computerized, so that the planning element is complemented by the possibility of follow-up and evaluation. Another process is the creation of interdepartmental teams on behalf of specific target populations. These teams are intended to conduct joint planning and coordinate between the different departments. Over the past year, three such interdepartmental teams were created by the municipality: a team that focuses on issues related to the elderly, another that concentrates on single-parent families and one that centres on youth in distress. The target populations themselves are also involved in the work of each of these three teams.

• Urban planning documents in our city reflect the interests of different social groups. The big attention is paid to children's interests. There is a well planned system of schools, nurseries, children's gardens as well as sports areas and playgrounds. For the elderly there is a planned system of care and elderly homes. All planning solutions are adapted to disabled persons.

• In the future there will be special goals for planning concerning different groups of people and impact analysis carried out to choose between different planning solutions.

• To provide for the needs of different groups in the population of our town, there are changing teams of planners, who work together on very special tasks for a certain time.

Intersectoral cooperation

One of the key indicators of the extent to which healthy urban planning is developing in cities is the level of contact between urban planning departments and healthy city projects. Informal contacts often stimulate opportunities to work jointly on specific projects, and this can lead to a joint approach throughout the process of planning in a city (Box 3.2). For example, in the Gasvej Neighbourhood planning project in Horsens (see Chapter 5), the urban planning department took the initiative to start the project, but it was also a key part of the Healthy City Project. In this way, close working links were developed between the two offices. In addition, the interdisciplinary steering group for the project brought on board representatives from education, social services and health departments as well as the residents of the area.

Initiatives in this area sometimes begin with the healthy city office assisting the urban planning department in certain areas of work, as in the example from Newcastle below, or with the urban planning department becoming involved in a project of the healthy city office, as in the example from Milan, above.

The survey of cities *(51)* asked whether urban planners had been involved in the work of the healthy city project. It shows a strong variation, as some cities had very good contact whereas others had none. Most cities surveyed had few links between the healthy city project and the urban planning department. Table 3.2 and Fig. 3.2 illustrate the results.

Table 3.2. Results of a survey of cities (n = 29) participating in the second phase of the WHO Healthy Cities project on cooperation with urban planners in the activities of healthy city projects

Category	Questionnaire responses	Number of cities	% of cities
Regular cooperation with urban planners	Yes, since the beginning of the healthy city project office Yes – continuous cooperation	7	24
Occasional cooperation with urban planners	Yes, for some projects Yes, only for preliminary planning Yes, in some cases Yes, for the Urban Child Project Yes, but only recently	14	48
No cooperation with urban planners	It does not include our work Not directly No	7	24
Other	No, but we have integrated the principles into our projects	1	3

Fig. 3.2.   Results of a survey of cities (n = 29) participating in the second phase
of the WHO Healthy Cities project on cooperation with urban planners
in the activities of healthy city projects

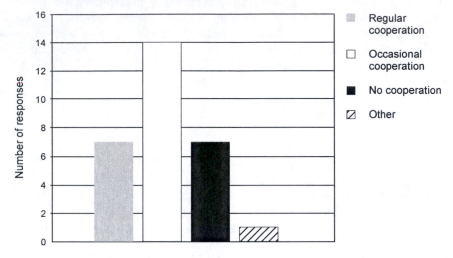

Four types of cooperation have been identified from questionnaire responses:

*   regular cooperation: implies a good understanding of links between health and
    urban planning issues;
*   occasional cooperation: implies an acknowledgement that there are some links
    between health and urban planning issues;
*   no cooperation: implies no acknowledgement of the links between health and
    urban planning issues; and
*   other: answers not included in the above groups but giving some significant
    information.

The comments from cities provide further insight into the different levels of contact.

*   Some suitable ideas and projects from the city architect's office are implemented
    or supported by our colleagues from the Healthy City office. For example, the
    idea of a trail through the conservation areas located in several city districts
    came from the city architect and was made possible by the Healthy City office.
*   I am a member of the cross-sectoral healthy city group which supports health
    promotion projects and Agenda 21 strategies initiated by citizens,
    nongovernmental organizations and others on a local level. This work has
    influenced the strategic municipal planning process and its implementation.
*   Colleagues in the planning department are involved in the healthy cities project
    in several ways. One is a member of the advisory body for the healthy cities
    project, one works on guidelines for the evaluation of municipal activities for

Box 3.2.   Intersectoral cooperation in the development of a new
strategic plan for Brno (Czech Republic)

In 1997 the Assembly of City Representatives of Brno approved the
preparation of a new strategic plan – a strategy for Brno. This plan is a tool
for the long-term strategic development of Brno, and incorporates economic,
social and environmental issues. It provides not only a vision for Brno, but
an agenda, action plan, and financial plan for realizing that vision. When
complete, the strategy will feed into the new master plan (strategic land-use
plan) for Brno.

Within the framework of the Healthy City Project, Brno has already begun
the process of planning, implementation and monitoring of activities aimed at
improving the health, conditions and quality of life of the people of Brno. In
keeping with the principles of the WHO strategy for health for all and the
principles of sustainable development, intersectoral cooperation has always
been a key element of this strategy. The principles of the Healthy City Project
are being integrated into the corporate vision of the city (strategy for Brno) so
that health is not considered a separate concept by the different sectors in the
city.

Within the Municipality of Brno, the urban planning department has been
designated as a coordination unit for the preparation of the strategy.
Representatives therefore form part of the coordination group, which also
includes politicians, members of other municipal departments, community
representatives and the Healthy City Project. The main task of this group
has been to establish working principles and a model for the development of
the strategy and to identify organizational changes in the structure of the
municipality that would facilitate the implementation of the strategy. A number
of open fora and round-table discussions have been organized to involve
both public and other professionals in producing the strategy. The key
principles for the development of the strategy, approved by the Assembly of
City Representatives, were as follows:

- sustainable development as a balance of economic, social and
  environmental development;
- active political support;
- a partnership approach;
- public participation; and
- continuous evaluation of the process.

As a result of this process, the coordination group has proposed a number of changes to the way the City Council is organized in Brno. The Municipality is currently considering the establishment of a new development unit, which will consist of part of the present urban planning department, the finance department and the Healthy City Project office. This organizational change is intended to address the links between urban planning and the Healthy City Project, providing an opportunity to integrate the WHO strategy for health for all and sustainable development into the strategic urban planning process.

Source: adapted from a presentation by Ivana Draholova, Brno Healthy City Project Coordinator, at the WHO Seminar on Healthy Urban Planning, Milan, Italy, 17–18 October 1999 (49,50).

children as part of an interdisciplinary group, and one does the same for the target group of disabled people. Another example is our involvement in a reduction programme for CO_2 emission and projects in relation to the Local Agenda 21 process.

Community involvement

Community participation in decision-making and implementation processes is a core element of the Healthy Cities approach. There are many examples of community participation in city health planning and in specific technical elements of the Healthy Cities project across Europe (38). Chapter 2 introduces the principle of community participation and its implications for urban planning. These ideas are developed in a practical sense in Chapter 5, but to what extent do urban planning processes currently involve effective community participation?

The cities were asked what the role of the citizen or consumer was in the urban planning process (51). Urban planning practices included three types of participation process:

- participatory: citizens cooperate with planners in all cases, supplying information and solutions that are taken into consideration;
- semi-participatory: citizens cooperate with planners only in some cases, supplying information and solutions that are taken into consideration; and
- nonparticipatory: the citizens' opinions have no real influence on the plan or project choices.

Table 3.3 illustrates these results. It shows that the culture of participation varies widely, with practices almost evenly distributed between the three approaches. Some cities have clearly made great inroads in this area, whereas in others, the urban planning process could benefit greatly from incorporating the Healthy Cities approach.

Table 3.3.   Results of a survey of cities (n = 29) participating in the second
phase of the WHO Healthy Cities project on the degree of citizen
participation in urban planning

Category	Questionnaire responses	Number of cities	% of cities
Participatory	Participation in the planning process Effective participation in all planning phases: draft and final plan	11	38
Semi-participatory	Active participation in some cases For short-term choices, citizen consensus is obligatory Certain groups are consulted on plans	7	23
Nonparticipatory	Citizens are informed by the publication of the plan Opportunities for public discussion and comment before adoption, petition afterwards The citizen can express his or her opinion on choices already formulated without any decision-making power The citizen has the right to see all the planning documentation Citizens are consulted by means of surveys and district meetings	11	38

The following extracts from the responses to the survey give an insight into the
variety of approaches to community participation in the urban planning process.

- Active participation in reaching joint solutions to urban issues and problems;
  feedback on performance of the local authority (user panels, citizens' panel);
  citizen role – taking responsibility for reporting issues and problems, for
  participating and voting.
- Interested citizens, organizations etc. have a great possibility to intervene through
  the planning process, i.e. through a preliminary "call for ideas" process, public
  hearings and meetings, through study groups, through direct collaboration with
  municipality staff.
- Citizens are involved both in the preparation and discussions regarding the
  proposal for land-use plans. In this process they can comment on proposed
  plans or initiate changes both in the role of citizen and owner.
- Citizens are consulted in the course of public enquiries and by means of urban
  district commissions. There is a green telephone number (city hot line) which
  citizens can call free of charge with views and requests.

Urban planners in some cities are already beginning to work with healthy city projects to improve their processes of community participation. In 1991, the Newcastle Healthy City project began a collaboration with the local urban planning department as part of the city's master planning and strategic planning process *(53)*. The project helped to publicize the draft plan to residents of the city by:

- making staff available to visit community groups to describe the proposals and seek their views;
- rewriting the draft document so that specific proposals for each community were brought together; and
- organizing events for particular interest groups, for example, young people and people with mental health problems *(53)*.

This provided the basis for ongoing collaboration in specific areas, for example in relation to cycling facilities and to a development proposal in the north of the city.

Box 3.3.   The Jerusalem Association of Community Councils
and Centers (Israel)

The Jerusalem Association of Community Councils and Centers (JACC) is an umbrella organization for 29 community councils and centres throughout Jerusalem. Its purpose is to strengthen Jerusalem's neighbourhoods by encouraging resident participation in improving the quality of life. The association works in close cooperation with the Healthy City Project, and the community councils have become the primary agencies for promoting and implementing health for all and Agenda 21 at the local level. The JACC is also affiliated with the municipality of Jerusalem.

The community councils are active in both Jewish and Arab neighbourhoods. Each one is run by a democratically elected board and consists of several committees, including a planning committee. The councils employ professional staff according to their needs and available facilities. Activities are wide ranging, and include preschool child care, leisure activities, educational and cultural activities and a number of activities more closely related to urban planning. The councils are involved in: identifying neighbourhood needs, developing neighbourhood plans and programmes, traffic and noise issues, parks and recreational facilities, recycling and ecology, and urban renewal – including improving derelict buildings and their surrounding areas and preserving older buildings.

The transfer of an increasing number of tasks to the community councils is part of a wider decentralization process in Jerusalem, and the JACC encourages people to take part in and support decentralized planning processes and neighbourhood initiatives. Citizen demands through the community centres have led to direct changes in the physical fabric of the neighbourhoods and in the planning policies applied in neighbourhoods. For example, the Nachlaot Rechavia community council represents a large group of elderly citizens. The Healthy City Project received numerous complaints from local residents pointing out that an increasingly large number of offices were moving into the neighbourhood. Many residents felt that the streets had become deserted at night, and they felt unsafe walking around outdoors. The community council, in cooperation with the municipality, passed a zoning resolution restricting the number of commercial enterprises allowed to locate in the area.

In summary, the activities of the community councils and the Healthy City Project in Jerusalem have transformed how the city thinks about local government. The councils have become a mechanism to increase grassroots involvement, promote equity on a practical and direct level, increase efficiency, reduce bureaucracy, save valuable resources, develop local leadership and empower residents on a range of issues that affect their lives.

Source: Waschitz *(54)*

DEVELOPING THE CONCEPT OF HEALTHY URBAN PLANNING IN CITIES

Understanding the concept of healthy urban planning, and all that it implies, is key to changing practice so that urban planning promotes the health and wellbeing of a city's people. To establish the extent to which urban planners in network cities think about health, specific questions were asked relating to:

- the links between health and urban planning;
- the meaning of healthy urban planning;
- current unhealthy practices;
- how urban planning can become healthier;
- how respondents would define a "healthy" outcome of urban planning work; and
- whether local health indicators could be integrated into and influence the urban planning process.

The following sections examine the results of these questions. They show that, although health may be implicit in urban planning considerations, urban planners are still not very conscious of health as an issue, and this underlines the need for a new focus within the urban planning profession. With a stronger health focus, urban planning can respond more holistically and effectively to today's challenges.

Links between health and urban planning

Chapter 1 outlines the links between health and urban planning, and Duhl & Sanchez *(2)* explored these in detail. Until now, however, urban planners have only really acknowledged a small proportion of these links. The survey of urban planners *(51)* found that many urban planners think about links to health primarily in terms of measures for reducing vehicular traffic and other environmental issues. Despite the variety of other ideas and principles acknowledged by planners in the survey, in practical terms, many continued to understand health in cities as an environmental problem and, more specifically, a pollution problem.

Respondents were asked to identify the greatest contribution urban planning could make to health. Table 3.4 indicates the range of areas identified. Some respondents identified more than one issue as important. The responses were categorized as follows: transport, public spaces and facilities, housing, preserving environmental and cultural heritage, urban planning models, the planning process and residential areas and neighbourhoods. The percentages are based on a total of 56 responses, and the results are summarized in Fig. 3.3.

Fig. 3.3.   Results of a survey of cities (n = 29) participating in the second phase of the WHO Healthy Cities project on the greatest contribution urban planning can make to health

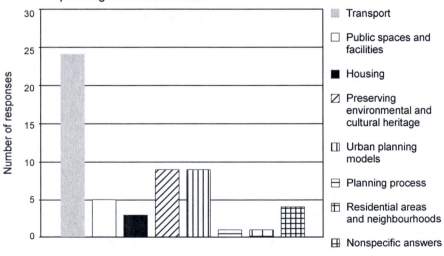

Table 3.4.   Results of a survey of cities (n = 29, 56 total responses) participating in the second phase of the WHO Healthy Cities project on the greatest contribution urban planning can make to health

Questionnaire responses		Number	% of responses
Transport		24	43
Public transport	5		
Cycling paths	3		
Traffic regulation	6		
Roads where children can play	1		
Pedestrian areas	2		
Mobility reduction	1		
Preventing pollution	4		
Efficient network of transport and accessibility	1		
Reducing car use	1		
Public spaces and facilities		5	9
Parks and squares	1		
Green belts and green spaces	3		
Leisure areas	1		
Housing		3	5
Good-quality housing standards	2		
Housing planning	1		
Preserving environmental and cultural heritage	9		16
Restoring monuments	1		
Restoring historic centres	1		
Protecting flora and fauna	1		
Preserving natural resources	4		
Preventing pollution	1		
Wastewater treatment	1		
Urban planning models		9	16
Controlled and balanced development	1		
Using ecological materials	1		
Multifunctional zoning	2		
Sustainability	2		
Municipal facilities network	0		
Principles of urban ecology	1		
Maintenance of existing buildings	1		
Quiet and safe squares and roads	1		
Planning process		1	2
Dialogue between the level at which decisions are made and the local level	1		
Residential areas and neighbourhoods		1	2
Residential areas with local facilities	1		
Nonspecific answer (theoretical)		4	7

Despite the general preoccupation with transport and pollution, some cities acknowledged the importance of linking health to urban planning in a wider sense, as the following excerpts from their comments demonstrate.

- Physical planning can alleviate the pressure coming from different urban activities and functions on the health of citizens. Moreover, physical planning is the key factor enabling the sustainable management of the urban system.
- Measures to improve the environment in the public realm – for all (e.g. streetscape, physical access, transport access, improved urban quality).
- To meet the basic human needs for economic, ecological, social and cultural welfare of the city.
- To reduce unemployment by assisting in the creation of job opportunities and the creation of healthy living environments. Health statistics in parts of the city with high unemployment and poor housing conditions compare badly with more affluent parts of the city.
- Traffic planning and implementation, residence-planning, wastewater treatment, environment-related issues, sustainability among many others are all very important elements or factors concerning health.

The meaning of healthy urban planning

Chapter 1 defines and explains healthy urban planning. The practical implications of developing healthy urban planning processes are explored throughout. Part 2, in particular, explores the policies and actions that make up this process. The way that different urban planners interpret the concept of healthy urban planning has

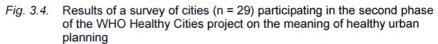

Fig. 3.4.   Results of a survey of cities (n = 29) participating in the second phase of the WHO Healthy Cities project on the meaning of healthy urban planning

Table 3.5.   Results of a survey of cities (n = 29, 44 total responses) participating in the second phase of the WHO Healthy Cities project on the meaning of healthy urban planning

Questionnaire responses	Number	% of responses
Traffic	**1**	**2**
Pedestrianized areas	1	
Public spaces and facilities	**4**	**9**
Pleasant urban spaces	3	
Leisure areas	1	
Housing	**2**	**5**
Better housing	2	
Interventions and guiding principles	**20**	**45**
Renewal of the urban centre	1	
Implies a holistic approach	1	
Can provide data and knowledge about health problems	1	
Similar to sustainable development	7	
Gives an emphasis on human society	2	
Relates to urban ecology	1	
Employment	1	
Avoiding monofunctional zoning	1	
Equal participation in the planning process	2	
Important for urban planners' education	1	
It influences lifestyles and depends on the economic situation	2	
Social structure	**3**	**7**
Reduction of social segregation	1	
Reduction of ghettoization	1	
Reduction of stress and loneliness	1	
Pollution	**4**	**9**
Reduction of pollution	3	
Reduction of noise	1	
Meaning unclear or answer theoretical or not specific	**11**	**25**

implications for practice in cities. It is therefore important, as work is developed in this area, to understand that planners have a variety of starting-points based on different organizational and institutional settings.

Respondents were asked whether the idea of healthy urban planning made sense to them. Table 3.5 and Fig. 3.4 illustrate how planners interpreted this concept. Responses were categorized into the following groups: traffic, public spaces and facilities, housing, interventions and guiding principles, social structure, and pollution. Since some respondents highlighted several issues, all are reflected in the tables. Percentages are therefore calculated based on 44 responses.

These results show that, overall, urban planners in WHO European network cities appreciated that the concept of healthy urban planning encompassed a wide range of issues. A number of respondents picked up on the social and economic aspects of the concept. However, the results also indicate that some people are preoccupied with the environmental and ecological aspects of sustainable development, and this can lead to a narrow interpretation of the concept of healthy urban planning.

Some cities identified key aspects of healthy urban planning.

- Healthy urban planning should create a physical environment that avoids or minimizes risk factors such as air pollution, noise, social segregation, loneliness, stress and the exclusion of any group (disabled, old people, refugees, children, poor people).
- Healthy urban planning means that the planning process must relate to the widest range of issues regarding health, as defined by the healthy cities project. Doing so will increase awareness of health-related issues among planners and decision-makers and ensure that it is a major consideration when they come to determine policy and set priorities. Of course, it is vital that the public be made similarly aware of these issues.
- My vision for our city would be an urban area devoid of litter, pollution, that is well maintained, that is free from exhaust fumes, that has pleasant urban spaces, both green and hard, free from derelict buildings and land, where people have jobs and decent houses and environments to live in, where the historic heritage of the city is reused by new industries and technologies. That is a healthy city.
- Healthy urban planning is today a truism, because urban planning without the aspect of health is nonsense.
- Practically every plan has positive and/or negative effects on people's health in the society. It is important that all plans are chosen in a way that their effects are as healthy as possible.

What is unhealthy in current urban planning practices?

If healthy urban planning is an ideal, a way of working to which urban planners should aspire, what is currently unhealthy about the way cities are planned? Many aspects of urban planning today could be labelled unhealthy. Some of these are identified in Chapter 1. Table 3.6 provides an overview of the opinions of urban planners in the network cities on this subject. Some respondents interpreted this as a question of process and others of outcome.

The results are arranged according to the following categories: transport, urban form, accessibility and equity, legislation and urban planning tools, guiding principles, pollution and social structure. Since many respondents identified more than one issue, 54 responses are included. The responses that particularly emphasize the principles of HEALTH21 and the Healthy Cities approach are highlighted in italics. Ten responses (19%) highlighted such principles. A further 17 (32%) focused on traffic and pollution problems.

Table 3.6.   Results of a survey of cities (n = 29, 54 total responses) participating in the second phase of the WHO Healthy Cities project on what is unhealthy in current urban planning practices

Questionnaire responses	Number	% of responses
Traffic	8	15
Vehicular traffic	7	
Excessive car use	1	
Urban form	6	11
High density	1	
Monofunctional zoning	2	
Derelict areas	1	
Contaminated land	2	
Accessibility and equity	3	6
Lack of open spaces	2	
Lack of diversity	1	
Legislation and urban planning tools	4	7
Inadequate legislation for public spaces	1	
Rigid plan	1	
Nonexistent plan	1	
Plan has not been implemented	1	
Guiding principles	9	17
Lack of attention to citizens' everyday needs	4	
Focus on short-term profit	2	
Predominance of private profit and a negative impact on the environment	3	
Pollution	9	17
Noise	2	
Air pollution	3	
Water pollution	2	
Waste	2	
Social structure	7	13
Social segregation	3	
Delinquency	1	
Drug abuse	1	
Unemployment	2	
No answer or nonspecific answer	8	15

The responses that emphasize the principles of HEALTH21 and the Healthy Cities approach are in italics.

The following extracts from survey responses provide a variety of perspectives on unhealthy planning practices from urban planners in the network cities.

• There are market demands for extensive urban developments (new shopping centres), which increases car traffic. Development of new separated residential areas and the renewal of neglected old housing areas in the city centre could open up the process of segregation of high- and low-income families. There has been nothing done with existing polluted areas – brownfields – in industrial parts of the city, which is a great threat for underground water and a healthy environment in general.

• The proliferation of sprawling low-density housing development, which results in traffic congestion and poor public transportation. The fact that transportation policies and land-use planning policies are largely uncoordinated. The lack of a clear policy in relation to open space provision for the city.

• A focus on short-term profits.

• Mostly it is a question of social environment (people who have many difficulties and problems have been put to live together in the same place) and unemployment.

• Occasionally, as a result of pressures from certain sectors of the population, entrepreneurs, and others, decisions do not reflect the importance of health factors.

Making processes healthier

This book provides many ideas and examples on how to create a healthy urban planning process, both guiding principles (part one) and planning at the levels of settlements, neighbourhoods and individual projects (part two). An analysis of the views of urban planners in WHO European network cities shows the level of compatibility with these ideas.

Table 3.7 and Fig. 3.5 illustrate the variety of suggestions made in response to the question: "In practical terms, how do you think the process of planning could be healthier?". The responses are categorized to show the suggestions that focused

Fig. 3.5.   Results of a survey of cities (n = 29) participating in the second phase of the WHO Healthy Cities project on how to make the process of urban planning healthy

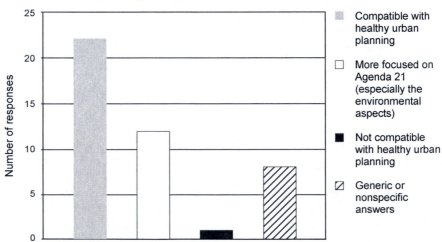

Table 3.7. Results of a survey of cities (n = 29, 43 total responses) participating
in the second phase of the WHO Healthy Cities project on how to
make the process of urban planning healthy

Questionnaire responses	Number	% of responses
Mostly compatible with healthy urban planning	**22**	**51**
Community participation in decision-making processes	4	
Developing a holistic vision for the city	3	
Involving the health department in the planning process	1	
Coordinating planning and implementation	1	
Traffic safety	1	
By considering the issue of health in planning	1	
By giving priority to health in decision-making	2	
Good regulation and urban planning standards	2	
Local decision-making powers for urban planning	1	
Not using cost as the determinant factor	1	
By using health monitoring techniques	1	
Creating social diversity in urban areas	1	
Greater understanding of the links between land use and lifestyles	2	
Long-term targets and step-by-step specifications	1	
More focused on Agenda 21 (especially the environmental aspects)	**12**	**28**
Application of Agenda 21	1	
Reduction of sprawl	4	
Promotion of public transport and bicycling	1	
More attention to environmental protection	2	
Reduction of pollution	2	
Coordinating land use and transport planning	1	
No zoning	1	
Not compatible with healthy urban planning	**1**	**2**
It is already healthy enough	1	
Generic or nonspecific answers	**8**	**19**

primarily on health or the Healthy Cities approach and the suggestions that more
strongly emphasized Agenda 21 principles. The links to Agenda 21 are difficult to
assess. In some cases the urban planner felt that healthy urban planning and Agenda
21 were one and the same process; in others, the respondents recognized that links
could be made and that there were opportunities for joint programmes, but this
was only part of the story. Since some cities gave more than one answer, the
percentages are calculated based on a total of 43 answers.

The examples below further indicate the variety of comments made about approaches to making urban planning processes healthier.

*   By making the link between land-use planning and healthier lifestyles more explicit, as well as the planning and economic arguments which are presented in favour or against specific proposals, the health benefits and disadvantages could be made clear.
*   By creating a planning and implementation process that includes citizen involvement and participation at a local level, dealing with local issues, tasks and possibilities and by connecting these efforts with general strategies.
*   Adequate demands regarding the environment, compromises between humans and the environment, not to live to its detriment; strengthening of environmental awareness, environmental education of citizens.
*   Let the urban health department play a role in the urban planning process. Sometimes radical projects (e.g. a car-free neighbourhood), more choices in favour of an optimum between social, economic and ecological interests.
*   By eliminating financial cost as the most important criterion, and by bearing in mind the resulting costs of social effects.

Defining healthy urban planning outcomes

This chapter has said much about principles and processes in healthy urban planning, but what about healthy urban planning outcomes? In Chapter 1, the examination of the 12 key health objectives of planning includes suggestions for healthy urban planning outcomes under each theme area, and these are developed in the second part of this book. The survey *(51)* also asked respondents to consider how they

Fig. 3.6.   Results of a survey of cities (n = 29, 39 total responses) participating in the second phase of the WHO Healthy Cities project on how healthy urban planning outcomes should be defined

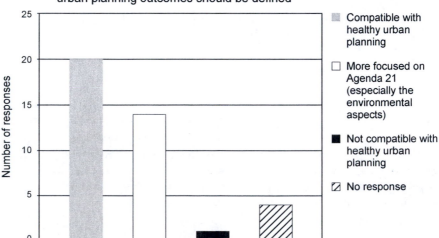

Table 3.8.   Results of a survey of cities (n = 29, 39 total responses) participating in the second phase of the WHO Healthy Cities project on how healthy urban planning outcomes should be defined

Questionnaire responses	Number	% of responses
Mostly compatible with healthy urban planning	**20**	**51**
When it is suitable to the needs of all groups	6	
When people are involved in influencing their future	1	
Housing improvements	1	
Introduction of specific standards	1	
A holistic approach	1	
Using better monitoring systems	4	
The improvement of health and social tension	1	
Structured infilling of the urban area to create a mix of uses	1	
Public green spaces	1	
Concerted implementation of planned choices	1	
Making politicians take responsibility	1	
Better quality of life in all urban areas	1	
More focused on Agenda 21 (especially the environmental aspects)	**14**	**36**
Well balanced	1	
Reduction of pollution	4	
Protection of historical heritage	2	
Balanced use of built areas and buildings	2	
Reduction of traffic	3	
Reduction of energy consumption	1	
Reduction of the use of natural resources	1	
Not compatible with healthy urban planning	**1**	**3**
Well defined zoning	1	
No response	**4**	**10**

The responses that are most significant in relation to healthy urban planning are indicated in italics.

would define the outcome of a planning exercise as healthy. The results are illustrated in Table 3.8 and Fig. 3.6. Similar to the previous question, the responses are categorized in terms of their overall compatibility with the concept of healthy urban planning, and a comparison is made to Agenda 21. Percentages are calculated based on a total of 39 identifiable responses. The responses that are most significant in relation to healthy urban planning are indicated in italics.

The comments below are among those that were most in line with the WHO concept of healthy urban planning. What they have in common is that, unlike some responses, they focus on the needs of the population and how they are affected by the physical, social and economic environment and the role the urban planner plays in determining that environment. In order for urban planning activities to be healthy, the outcome needs to be viewed in terms of people; healthy urban planning begins with people.

- The outcome of a planning exercise can be defined as healthy if it can ensure all the following conditions:
  - the upgrading of the living conditions for every citizen and for the next generations;
  - the upgrading of the local economy in a continuous way, with regard to the future; and
  - the protection of the natural, cultural, historical and architectural heritage.
- Structured filling-in of the urban and open (green) area so that living in every part of the city becomes pleasant again; the school safe and the shops nearby, the playground on the corner, the workplace nearby, the open space visible and perceptible. Accessibility also stands for safety of cyclists and pedestrians and presence of public transport.
- A well thought-out planning process should make it possible not only to improve the physical health of the population but also to increase their level of socialization and the integration of individuals into the community.
- Criteria of healthy environments: they are adapted to the needs of population as regards social contacts, security of life and property, and access to recreation areas, services and shops etc. Criteria of healthy populations: people's needs are met.

Fig. 3.7.   Results of a survey of cities (n = 29) participating in the second phase of the WHO Healthy Cities project on whether health indicators can be integrated into and influence the urban planning process

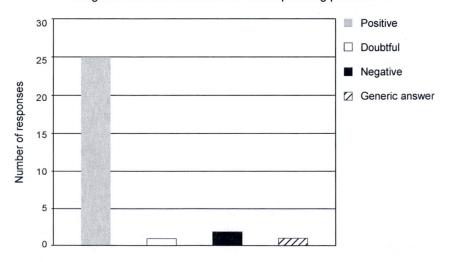

• We would define planning as being healthy when it meets the needs of all groups, children families, youth, elderly people and last but not least, disabled persons.

Use of indicators in the urban planning process

The WHO Healthy Cities project uses indicators as a core element of its health planning process. Chapter 2 discusses the use of indicators, and Annex 3 contains the indicators used during the second phase of the project. Annex 3 identifies the indicators that are normally used in urban planning. The questionnaire asked urban planners whether they felt that health indicators (describing the health of the population and the state of the social and environmental factors that influence health) could be integrated into and influence the urban planning process.

The responses are illustrated in Table 3.9 and Fig. 3.7, and categorized into: positive, doubtful, negative and not significant. Since only one response was possible per city, the percentages represent the proportion of cities responding.

Since this question was unequivocal, its meaning should have been clear to all respondents. The respondents widely accepted introducing health indicators into the analytical phase of preparing urban plans. Further, some planners view the indicators as a useful tool in supporting plan choices and in measuring outcomes. The following are extracts from some of the positive questionnaire responses.

Table 3.9.   Results of a survey of cities (n = 29) participating in the second phase of the WHO Healthy Cities project on whether health indicators can be integrated into and influence the urban planning process

Questionnaire responses	Number	% of cities
Positive	**25**	**86**
Yes, if they are used to monitor planning outcomes	1	
Yes, needed for planning decision-making and monitoring	12	
Yes, it is possible	2	
Yes, they are important	7	
Yes, to explain changes to people	1	
Yes, they are already being used in some cases	2	
Doubtful	**1**	**3**
Perhaps, in ideal situations	1	
Negative	**2**	**7**
No, only a few of them	2	
Generic answer	**1**	**3**

- Yes, it has great importance.
- They should be integrated in the planning process because health is a determinant of city planning. Literature, conferences should be developed on that subject in order to make everybody aware that "planning my city is planning my health".
- Local health indicators should be included in local plans and project documents. They would be helpful in providing the context against which policies and proposals should be set. A process of monitoring the effects of policies would then be possible.
- Health indicators make it possible to provide a common pool of knowledge about the health status of the population, to track changing needs and to prepare appropriate responses. They are essential to any decision-making. They provide an evaluation tool in planning health activities and a communication tool in contacts between various administrative services, associations and the general population.
- Yes – when these factors and indicators are published and are the ground for appreciation by politicians and municipal government.

CONCLUSIONS

The results of the survey of the urban planning departments of the 38 cities participating in the second phase of the WHO Healthy Cities project provide an opportunity to compare the recommendations made in Chapters 1 and 2 with the current situation. This information allows an assessment of the extent to which the Healthy Cities approach has begun to permeate urban planning policy and practice. The following conclusions can be drawn.

To most respondents, the concept of a healthy city seems to be intuitively clear. In many ways, the desire for improving health is an implicit aspect of urban planning systems, and enthusiasm was significant for a healthy approach to urban planning that had people's quality of life and wellbeing as its central purpose. This is not surprising, given the historic links between the public health and urban planning movements.

However, in general terms, people's understanding of the extent to which health and urban planning are linked is limited, and this has led to fragmented theoretical and practical interpretations of healthy urban planning: many respondents reproduced the traditional planning approach with overgeneralization (no consideration of specific needs) or overspecialization (focusing on marginal projects rather than a holistic approach).

There is wide diversity in interpretation, and consequently in the implementation of HEALTH21 and Healthy Cities principles. In particular, the links with the environmental aspects of sustainable development and the Agenda 21 process tend to be overemphasized. Sustainable development is a key principle of HEALTH21 and Healthy Cities, and it is misleading and limiting to view sustainability primarily in environmental terms. Many respondents gave priority to environmental questions, almost exclusively focusing on private car traffic. Although some respondents acknowledged the social determinants of health, they were overlooked by many respondents.

The principles promoted by WHO have led to some important local innovations in urban planning, both at a strategic and local level, but the general impact remains limited. In fact, most municipal administrations do not seem to have succeeded in incorporating health principles into the planning process. They instead tend to place health-related initiatives in marginal areas and consider them as "interesting projects".

Healthy urban planning is a new area of work, both the concept and its implications for planning and managing cities. It reflects the infective nature of the Healthy Cities approach, that, even before healthy urban planning became a formal requirement, some cities had made significant progress in developing it. Their experience will be greatly valued as WHO develops its initiative to promote healthy urban planning and as more and more cities embrace this approach both in cities participating in the WHO network and beyond.

Part two

Guidelines for healthy urban planning

Chapters 4–6 introduce the practice of healthy urban planning. They examine, in turn, settlements as a whole, neighbourhoods within a settlement and specific development projects. Each chapter starts with guidance on philosophy and process and then moves on to key policy areas and ends with one or two case studies. Chapter 6, on projects, is distinctive in being cast as a checklist of questions to assist in improving project proposals and in evaluating projects.

Chapter 4

Settlement planning: making towns and cities good places to live

PURPOSE AND SCOPE

This chapter is intended to provide guidance for urban planners when they are faced with the problem of planning whole towns and cities. It could be helpful in a range of situations:

- devising long-term strategic land-use or transport plans;
- seeing strategies for specific topics in context, including those for housing, employment, retailing, energy or water; and
- selecting locations for new development.

The emphasis is on the spatial development of cities – which is the key responsibility of the planner. However, the planning of space is inseparable from other social, economic and resource issues. The chapter is structured to draw out these relationships.

It adopts the ecosystem approach suggested by the European Sustainable Cities & Towns Campaign and uses this to recommend a simple technical planning process in five stages. This reasonably systematic and rational process is compatible with the Healthy Cities approach to urban management. It should underpin and inform the collaboration and decision-making process if health objectives are to be achieved. The main part of the chapter provides guidance on the broad policy areas of urban form, jobs and facilities, housing, transport and resources.

AN ECOSYSTEM APPROACH: CREATING SETTLEMENTS THAT PROVIDE A HEALTHY HUMAN HABITAT

The chapter deals with strategic planning issues at the scale of the whole town or city or of an urbanized region with a number of interdependent settlements. It starts from the premise that planning healthy settlements requires seeing the urban area in functional ecological terms, reflecting the daily patterns of human activity, rather than defining it by physical edges or administrative boundaries. The problems of poor air quality, poor accessibility and social polarization can only be effectively tackled when the dependent commuting hinterland of a city or urban cluster is brought into the equation. This area is referred to here as a city region.

Since municipal administrative units responsible for transport, energy, water and health often do not coincide either with the city region or each other, making coherent policies is very difficult. Neighbouring authorities and related agencies must therefore collaborate and ensure a consistent approach.

One key to consistency is a shared planning philosophy. This can be provided by the ecosystem approach. Settlements in their hinterlands are seen as ecosystems, different human groups and activities are interdependent and the relationship with the resource base of land, air, water, energy, food and materials is made explicit (Fig. 4.1). The shared objective, overriding the specific agency remits, is to create a healthy human habitat functioning to create opportunities and a high quality of environment for people irrespective of wealth or status and in a manner that is ecologically sustainable.

Establishing this shared philosophy and consequent commitment to partnership are prerequisites for effective action.

The strength of the ecosystem approach is its capacity to treat settlements holistically. Its weakness can be the temptation to treat each city region as an independent entity. This has occurred, for example, in the south of England. Certain authorities in the recent past have estimated the maximum population an area can support without unacceptably compromising health and environmental quality and

Fig. 4.1.   Monitoring the settlement as an ecosystem

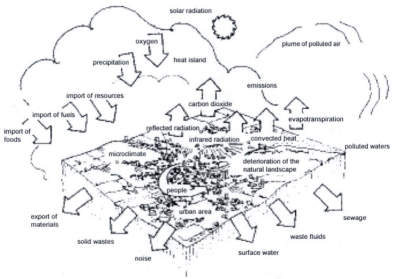

1. Have the input and output of the settlement been audited?
2. How can unsustainable input and output be reduced?

Source: Barton et al. *(55)*

then "pulled up the drawbridge", refusing to permit further development. But no city is an island. Given contemporary levels of mobility and the global marketplace, the city's ecosystem nests within wider regional and global ecosystems that define its role in part.

AGENCY REMITS AND THE NEED FOR COOPERATION

Many systems of urban planning and management in Europe rely on specialist agencies pursuing their particular remits largely in isolation. For example, there are often separate agencies for transport, pollution control, energy, water, health and land development. These systems are failing. They are based on an overly simplistic linear view of cause and effect and an outmoded competitive ideology. The necessity for a holistic and integrated approach means that cooperation and partnership must replace competition. The most critical spheres for cooperation are:

- land-use and transport planning, linking the planning for the location of housing, employment and facilities with a strategy for transport;
- strategies for social services, embracing the forward planning for social housing, health, education, library services, public open space and other public services with integrated land-use and transport planning;
- economic regeneration strategies, so that economic development and urban regeneration programmes are means of implementing a healthy planning strategy;
- an integrated transport strategy, incorporating road construction and maintenance, road traffic management, car-parking, rail service, planning and operating public transport, planning of bicycle and moped transport and providing for pedestrian transport; and
- integrated resource planning, maximizing the opportunities for synergistic solutions involving energy, water, food, waste, wildlife, job creation and recreation strategies (Box 4.1).

Working jointly, or even just sharing information, across all these different spheres of policy-making is an intimidating prospect. Some agencies may have remits that cut across effective collaboration. For example, energy supply industries may be required to satisfy demand rather than be concerned with minimizing unhealthy emissions or increasing the ability of less affluent people to obtain fuel. In some countries, healthy urban planning may depend on governments changing these remits. But a shared concern for the health of the city can be a powerful motivator for cooperation. The rest of the chapter takes partnership as a given.

Box 4.1.   An ecosystem approach in Hammarby Sjöstad, Stockholm
(Sweden)

Hammarby Sjöstad, a major development project for an extension to
Stockholm's southern area, Södermalm, is planned such that the normal
environmental impact of the building project is halved. This process is intended
to apply to both the construction phase and the subsequent living
arrangements. The technical supply is being designed with the aim of
achieving mutually supporting and environmentally effective solutions for
energy, water, wastewater and waste.

A partnership comprising the city authorities and the three main water,
energy and waste-management companies developed a joint concept for
the new district that will be resource efficient and exploit the maximum
recycling technology.

Stockholm Vatten AB (Stockholm Water Company) produces and supplies
drinking-water and manages wastewater treatment plants and reservoirs
across Sweden; Skafab, owned by the City of Stockholm, will have the primary
responsibility for solid waste management, and Stockholm Energi AB is one
of Sweden's leading energy suppliers.

The planned new development centres around an old industrial estate next
to a harbourside area and will contain approximately 8000 apartments for
about 15 000 people. New buildings will be constructed in districts with a
mixture of housing, shops, offices and small businesses. The buildings will
be four to six storeys high and situated along the contours of the land. The
buildings will provide balconies, terraces and outdoor spaces with views
across the water.

The aim is to create ecological cycles at as local a level as possible by:

- minimizing the consumption of natural resources;
- using energy from renewable sources, and based on local sources as
  much as possible;
- tailoring solutions to residents' needs by promoting social cooperation
  and ecological responsibility and by encouraging public participation in
  shaping the district; and
- developing projects that should act as a lever to develop new solutions
  for using energy and other natural resources, promoting local food
  production, reusing and recycling waste products and minimizing the
  demand for transport.

An environmental information centre run by the three companies will help to provide information and resources as the project develops. The diagram below illustrates the energy, water and waste flows.

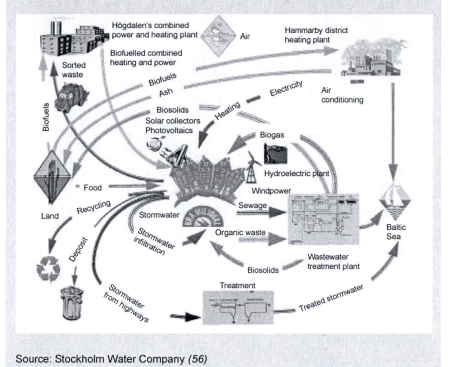

Source: Stockholm Water Company *(56)*

A STRATEGIC PLANNING PROCESS: COLLABORATIVE, SYSTEMATIC AND OPEN

Strategic environmental assessment

The model of the strategic planning process given here is derived from two main sources: the emerging European Union requirements for strategic environmental assessment and the collaborative interagency process pioneered by the Healthy Cities movement. The latter is fully explored in Chapter 2. The final strategic environmental assessment directive is still being adopted, but various forms of strategic environmental assessment, applied specifically to land-use plans, are in operation in countries such as Germany, the Netherlands and the United Kingdom. In its full form, strategic environmental assessment not only rigorously evaluates plans when they emerge, but focuses on the entire process by which plans are produced. Key aspects are clarity of objectives, reporting on the state of the environment, effective policy scoping and testing of alternative strategies. Strategic

Fig. 4.2. The idealized process of making policy through planning

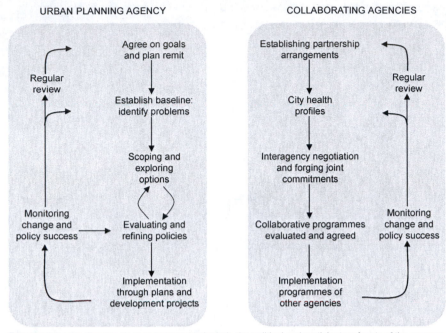

For simplicity, the diagram does not attempt to include the political and participatory facets of the process.

Source: Barton et al. *(17)*

environmental assessment is reinforcing the importance of an honest, explicit and transparent approach to making plans.

Several governments and many local authorities are actively developing the principles of strategic environmental assessment into the more rounded idea of strategic sustainability assessment, explicitly incorporating social and economic criteria as well as environmental ones. Health implications should be a key part of such assessment. One motivation for initial collaboration between agencies responsible for planning, health and other sectors could be the need to establish a common baseline – a joint city health profile (Chapter 2). This forms a key stage in the strategic planning process (Fig. 4.2).

A five-stage process
1. Negotiate clear goals and the remit of the plan
Having joint working practices and shared responsibility is not often practical at the onset of a plan-making process. Nevertheless, consulting widely with agencies, the public and politicians on the broad purpose and scope of the plan is vital. Creating a healthier city is an aim on which all interests can agree. It puts the current and future quality of life of the people of the city at centre stage. Other

objectives, about jobs, housing, transport, resources and environment, can flow from it. Community visioning and social attitude surveys are explored in detail in *Community participation in local health and sustainable development: a working document on approaches and techniques (38)*. These can provide a valuable input to the process of defining priorities.

The remit of the plan needs to be set such that the plan can effectively address creating a healthier city. Without invading the territory of other agencies, that plan needs to be recognized as the means by which the spatial decisions of all the relevant public, private and voluntary bodies are negotiated to be consistent and mutually reinforcing.

2. Establishing the baseline: problems and opportunities
Common ground and understanding between varied interests is top priority if later implementation is to be successful. Joint programmes designed to establish the baseline social, health, economic and environmental conditions (in the form of a city health profile) can be a relatively objective and nonpolitical way of recognizing the problems experienced by specific groups or communities. General agreement that there are certain problems that need to be addressed is an important step in forging alliances to do something about it.

Spatial policy-making can only, however, tackle certain kinds of problems. False expectations must not be raised. That is one reason why the city health profile should be owned by all the main policy agencies, so that each plays their role in response.

The analysis must also deal with the interests of future generations as well as the present one. Expected pressures for commercial development, predicted problems of congestion, housing quality, inequity and other problems should emerge clearly. A simple but powerful analytical framework is pressure, state and response.

- **Pressure**. How are commerce, technology and lifestyles changing and how will this affect health?
- **State**. What is the current and projected state and quality of environmental, economic and social capital?
- **Response**. What policies are in place and how effective are they in tackling problems?

3. Scoping and exploring options
Although establishing the baseline is important for a long-term and evolving project, effective policy is needed immediately. So scoping and policy development need to proceed at the same time that problems are being identified and analysed. Each can inform the other. Indeed, a particular proposal can often trigger further survey work. The process has to be pragmatic, given limited resources and political pressures.

Scoping the plan and exploring options go hand in hand. The European Union's process of strategic environmental assessment as applied to spatial plans mandates an obligation to cast the net wide by looking at best practices and innovative ideas in other municipalities, at European Union and government advice and the local process of consultation with relevant agencies.

The purpose of examining alternatives is to overcome policy inertia and to encourage every authority to innovate. The apparent absence of realistic options in many policy-making processes is always suspicious. It leads to the suspicion that established interests (market, institutional or political) have commandeered the exercise and inhibited open discussion.

4. Evaluating and refining policies

The process of evaluating and choosing policy has to be open, explicit and transparent if the resulting decisions are to carry weight. Quantitative and qualitative assessments need to be balanced, and the interests of different groups (sometimes conflicting) need to be recognized. The original health and environmental objectives of the plan provide the criteria for judgement.

Fig. 4.3.   Sample matrix for assessing the compatibility of objectives, policies and proposals related to transport in a city region

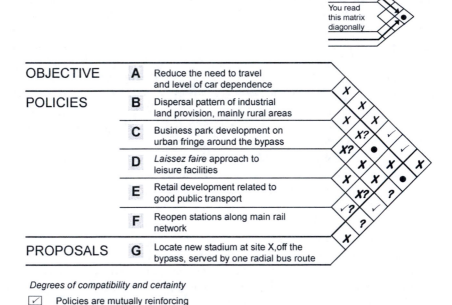

Degrees of compatibility and certainty

☑   Policies are mutually reinforcing

●   Policies have little or no mutual effect (neutral)

☒   Policies tend to undermine each other

?   Uncertain or unknown effects (may be applied with any of the other symbols)

Source: adapted from Barton & Bruder *(57)*

The real difficulty in evaluating is taking account of the interactive and cumulative effects of policy. One way of coping with real-life complexity is to use matrices to highlight areas of conflict and reinforcement between policies.

The matrix in Fig. 4.3 relates a broad objective to a range of policies of a local authority and to the proposals of other key agencies. This helps to establish norms of consistency in the negotiations between agencies and to encourage the authority to become more explicit in its internal decision processes. This is an example of a completed version.

5. Coordinating implementation

By themselves, many planning agencies have rather limited, mainly negative, powers. There is no value in bravely allocating land for housing if water, transport, economic development, health and education agencies are nowhere to be seen! The job of the planner is to negotiate and establish coordinated programmes of implementation in which the different agencies agree on the main social objectives. The goals of human health and quality of life provide a pivot for winning commitment. If these goals are backed at the highest level by politicians and chief officers, then fruitful partnerships can be sustained and social outcomes improved.

STRATEGIES FOR URBAN FORM: TOWARDS INTEGRATION, REGENERATION AND CONCENTRATION

The spatial relationship between different land uses helps to determine levels of car dependence, accessibility, community and equity. It is therefore vital that each land use not be treated as a separate planning problem, as this can result in a disaggregated and dispersed pattern. Avoiding the centralized imposition of overly simplistic zoning schemes that restrict choice and diversity is equally vital. A successful strategy for land use requires long-term commitment by a range of agencies.

Health priorities
The health priorities of any urban planning strategy include:

* to enhance accessibility by foot and bike and thus to promote healthy exercise and the sense of local community, increasing equity in the access to services for people with poor access to transport;
* to enhance the viability of public transport as a means of increasing travel options and cutting reliance on car use, hence reducing accidents, air pollution and CO_2 emissions;
* to increase the choices open to all sectors of the population – especially people who do not use cars – for access to employment, education, health, shopping and leisure activities;

- to increase the range and quality of residential accommodation, and thus to facilitate households finding housing to suit their needs and income; and
- to foster the economic buoyancy of settlements, increasing the range of job opportunities and creating the resources needed to both regenerate urban areas and provide services.

The debate on urban form

Urban form is defined here as the distribution and pattern of human settlement within the city region. The key variables are density, shape, degree of dispersal or concentration and the quality of the infrastructure for public transport. The debate about sustainable urban form is intense in academic circles, with powerful advocacy of different forms of compactness or decentralization. The consensus within the European Union countries favours the idea of urban compactness and hinterland restraint put forward by the 1990 *Green paper on the urban environment (58)*. The idea of compactness has fairly obvious health and sustainability benefits compared with a dispersed pattern – at least in theory:

- trip lengths are shorter (than a dispersed pattern) and there are more opportunities for exercise through walking and cycling;
- car dependence is lower, reducing levels of air pollution;
- a wide choice of facilities is within easy walking distance, promoting greater access to and choice of food;
- land values can be sufficient to encourage urban renewal and regeneration, which can help foster pride and a sense of community;
- the vitality and viability of the city centre is bolstered, improving the economy and providing more employment opportunities;
- buildings and materials are reused, reducing energy and resource consumption; and
- access to rural open space is improved, providing opportunities for increased recreational activity.

So compactness can potentially help achieve a cleaner, more accessible, more equitable and convivial environment. Nevertheless, compactness can create problems in terms of excessive density, loss of open space, high housing prices (leading to social exclusion) and implementation. If the rate of growth is high, the capacity of existing urban areas may not be sufficient. Further, car-oriented market pressures, weak legislation, inter-city competition for important development sites together with the poor image of some urban areas may make compact city development very difficult to achieve.

Each city region has its own unique social and economic dynamics, political pressures and geographical characteristics. No answer is therefore universal. Below are four urban form strategies policy-makers might consider: urban regeneration, compact growth, focused decentralization and linear concentration. These four options are organized as a sequential test, so that those that are healthiest in theory are examined first. They are options for urban development over 10–25 years. They are sequential in the sense that, only if urban regeneration proves unsatisfactory is it appropriate to move on to compact growth, and only if compact growth is inappropriate is it right to consider focused decentralization and linear concentration.

Strategy for urban regeneration

A strategy for urban regeneration relies on accommodating most new development (such as more than 80%) within the existing urban area, by reusing and recycling buildings and brownfield sites. If the city's housing and commercial property markets are buoyant, this strategy puts considerable pressure on urban open space and settlements that spill over the current city limits. It therefore relies on strong and effective planning policies if it is to work in the interests of the inhabitants (see case study, Box 4.2).

Checklist
- Is there capacity within the existing urban area for the predicted residential, commercial and service development through (for example) reclaiming derelict sites, redeveloping low-density uses and division of plots and houses?
- Is this theoretical spare capacity well located in relation to existing or planned job and service centres and public transport services, with isolated or poorly related urban zones excluded?
- Will normal market processes (decisions by firms and households) be able to deliver this intensification within the time scale needed?
- Are there current planning policies that unnecessarily inhibit intensification – for example, policies about maximum plot ratios (building density), minimum provision of parking or preserving the existing social character of an area?
- Have urban open spaces (in private as well as public ownership) used by local people or that have special ecological, aesthetic or historical value been identified and effectively protected from the development pressure?
- Have peripheral greenfield, satellite village sites and prime agricultural land (where development is often cheaper than in town) been effectively constrained to oblige developers to implement the strategy?
- Where brownfield land is contaminated or complex or expensive to redevelop, are there grants or partnership arrangements that can help lever in private money?

Box 4.2.   Regeneration in Barcelona (Spain): the renewal of a degraded district (Ciutat Vella)

The historical district of Ciutat Vella (91 000 inhabitants) was one of the most degraded areas and also had a very low socioeconomic status within the City of Barcelona. This included high general and specific death rates and high exposure to principal risk factors for poor health, such as violence, prostitution, AIDS, drug addiction and unhealthy housing. The growing decay also resulted from inadequate urban planning decisions and from the lack of a plan to provide the necessary regulations and set out a financial strategy.

The renovation plan, in line with the principles of the WHO Healthy Cities project, was realized by a cooperative that brought together a variety of public and private partners including the University of Barcelona, the Port of Barcelona, the regional and local governments, various service companies and firms together with a joint venture company (PROCIVESA) that represents the City of Barcelona. The public investment of US $80 million immediately attracted private investors. The achievements included: restoration and general improvement of dwellings, opening of squares and green spaces, building of cultural and recreational facilities, health programmes for groups on the margins of society and economic development programmes. More than a decade has passed, and the first results can now be seen and compared. The area has many new economic activities, and the present population enjoys a much improved socioeconomic status.

Source: WHO Regional Office for Europe *(6)*

The urban regeneration strategy applies especially to regions with moderate growth where economic restructuring is occurring or where current gross urban density is low. In some cities, existing high density may preclude intensification. However, the principle of recycling underused urban land and buildings applies to all strategies. It can be important in relation to towns and cities that are dying through experiencing economic and social decline and a consequent loss of population, as well as in rural areas where competition between towns is exacerbated by increasing concentration of retail outlets out of town.

Strategy for compact growth
A strategy for compact growth should be considered when the urban area has insufficient capacity to accommodate the growth predicted. The strategy then is to release land close to the city with good access to urban facilities by foot, bicycle

and public transport. Development on greenfield sites is not seen as an alternative to regeneration but as a supplement.

Checklist
- Do studies show clearly that the capacity of the existing urban area is insufficient to accommodate new development without compromising environmental quality or threatening long-term economic stability and social equity?
- Are there greenfield sites around the city that potentially provide a good level of accessibility by bike and public transport to the city centre (such as within 5 km) or by foot to a district centre (such as within 1.5 km) and provide an attractive environment for living and working?
- Can such sites be developed while preserving valued green space – in particular the flood plains, hill crests, woodlands and recreational parklands?
- Could the development of such sites be used to assist (rather than compete with) urban regeneration, for example by funding new health and educational facilities in part, improving access to dying industrial estates, justifying an improved suburban public transport service or triggering the renewal of a district centre?
- Have stakeholders in the existing urban zone (for example, residents' groups, service providers and commercial interests) been consulted to help establish how the new development could best assist in this way?

The compact growth strategy is likely to apply to cities that are growing more rapidly but are still relatively small. It is not appropriate or even possible for conurbations. Note that the 1.5-km standard relates to the distance many people are prepared to walk to reach a town centre. The encouragement of walking trips is an important health goal, but habits are different in each cultural area. Locally valid criteria must be devised that reflect human behaviour and the prevailing physical conditions.

Strategy for focused decentralization
A strategy for focused decentralization is a development of the strategy for compact growth that is adapted to the larger canvas, giving a focus for the decentralizing forces of the market. Research suggests that applying the compact strategy can become counterproductive if the city exceeds a certain size, since:

- daily trip lengths get too long;
- congestion and pollution are worsened;
- space competition becomes intense;
- access to open country is poor; and
- problems of social exclusion and polarization increase.

Further peripheral growth of major cities (perhaps over a 5-km radius or about 250 000 population) should therefore be viewed critically.

The focused decentralization strategy attempts to deflect some of the growth potential into suburban towns or free-standing commuter towns with the aim of making these more self-sufficient in jobs and services, effectively counter-magnets to the main city. The strategy is particularly appropriate for highly urbanized regions with clusters of closely linked cities.

Checklist
- Has the potential for urban intensification in the dominant city and nearby towns been fully recognized and researched, so that it forms a key part of any strategy?
- Is the city too extensive or populous to permit a compact growth strategy without unduly exacerbating the access, health and equity problems listed above?
- Are there nearby towns with centres that are (or could become) very accessible by public transport locally and regionally and that have the economic potential to provide a wide range of job opportunities and services?
- Are there greenfield sites in and around such centres that fulfil the criteria for compact growth?
- If existing towns offer inadequate opportunities for growth, is there the potential for a new town that is sufficiently far from the main city to establish its relative independence but yet attractive to major employers, and with excellent prospective connections for public transport?
- Can these growth towns (new or old) potentially provide a fair level of autonomy, with most employed residents working locally, and good services, including major food and clothing stores, a leisure centre or stadium, hospital, adult college (as well as schools), a library and theatre, cinemas and dance halls?

Linear concentration strategy

The focused decentralization strategy poses real difficulties. It performs well in theoretical modelling exercises in an imagined future in which the friction of distance is high, but it performs poorly in the current situation, in which the cost of fuel (in many countries) is relatively low, car ownership is rising and car use has been fostered by road building. People have many work, shopping, leisure and social options within a trip time of 30 minutes. In this situation, the decentralization strategy can simply increase the average length of trips and the dispersed pattern of trips, and spread the resulting dangers and poisons to a wider area.

So another option is to return to the idea of concentration, not on a peripheral pattern as before but instead linear. Linear concentration means growth along broad public transport corridors linking the dominant city and counter magnet centres. These corridors should not be too long, or the same problem of long trip lengths occurs as with the previous strategy.

The strength of the linear strategy is that it does not pretend that nearby towns can be functionally free-standing but rather treats the city region as an social and economic entity, while still encouraging localization.

Checklist
- Has the potential for urban intensification and compact development been fully explored and exploited?
- Would the focused decentralization strategy be likely to result (if fuel continues to be relatively inexpensive) in a dispersed pattern of long trips and significant reliance on cars?
- Are there opportunities close to the main city for developing the corridors along existing or proposed main routes for public transport, linking between the city and existing or potential subcentres?
- Can such corridors be broad enough (such as 1–2 km) to allow the development of local facilities along them and generate high demand for public transport?
- Can such a strategy be pursued without unduly exacerbating congestion on radial routes and without destroying the setting of historical towns or the sense of separate identity?

Conclusion

There are no quick fixes to the problem of devising a strategy for a healthy urban form. Politicians and academic pundits are often searching for clean, clear solutions, but the urban planner has to deal with fuzzy reality, creatively managing the problems raised by any general strategy without compromising the goals. Both the focused decentralization and the linear concentration strategies may be appropriate, singly or in combination, in different settings. Both fully embrace and then go beyond the regeneration and compact options.

LOCATION OF JOBS AND FACILITIES: PLANNING FOR MIXED USE

If the strategies to obtain a sustainable urban form are to succeed, then some control must be exercised over the location of business and institutional activities, which generate the demand for mobility. The potential health benefits in terms of air quality, safety, exercise, accessibility and equity are considerable.

The focus is on all activities that generate substantial trips for people or freight:

- retail, leisure and tourist facilities;
- office developments (public and private sectors);
- industrial and distribution facilities; and
- health, educational and cultural facilities.

All these activities need to be treated consistently in transport and land-use planning to reduce car use and foster walking, bicycling and the use of public transport while ensuring a high and equitable level of accessibility.

Cities with a weak economic base or poor levels of state support have fundamental difficulty in achieving this. Companies and public agencies aim to minimize costs and increasingly choose car-based locations, and both these considerations can point to edge-of-town sites. Restricting choice of location is politically and socially unacceptable if jobs are at stake and vital services are not provided. A framework of decision-making must therefore be created in which healthy decisions are also economically optimal.

Principles

- Awareness of health and environmental issues should be raised, for example, through city health profiles and high profile political and public activity, so that they become a common concern and publicly embarrassing for leaders of businesses and institutions to ignore.
- A collaborative Healthy Cities approach should be developed for business leaders and agency heads to establish common ground and work towards partnerships and shared policy visions.
- Sustainable patterns of land use should be promoted not only based on social, health and environmental benefits but also as an effective way of stimulating economic viability and agency effectiveness. Access should be improved for all groups, commerce will benefit by clustering activities, and the city can be marketed based on a healthier image and good quality of life.
- Comprehensive and consistent planning guidelines should be established that create a level playing field for all forms of business activity. In some countries, legislation needs to be changed or improved to enable this.
- Transport investment and policies to restrain car use should be used to focus business and agency attentions on appropriate locations and make inappropriate locations more costly: for example, by imposing an annual charge on parking spaces for private cars.

Distinguishing local from city-wide facilities

Some jobs and services are local in character; others serve a much wider catchment. Local facilities need to be dispersed across the city so they are accessible to local communities. In an unregulated market, major offices and superstores (with a district or regional catchment) are often sited in a dispersed location. These two sets of facilities needs to be treated very differently if public transport accessibility, which requires concentrated facilities, is a key criterion.

The different types and levels of service must be distinguished. Table 4.1 distinguishes four categories of location and identifies the kind of accessibility criteria that could be used to guide development.

Facilities serving a primarily local function (category D) should be clustered within the locality (increasing the opportunity for multi-purpose trips) and centrally located in relation to walking and bicycling networks.

All major trip generators serving a catchment greater than local (category B) should be concentrated at public transport nodes, where good access by public transport can be gained from most directions. Major facilities serving a city-wide or regional catchment (category A) should be located near intercity coach and rail services and at the heart of urban public transport services. These principles reaffirm

Table 4.1. Jobs and facilities: categories of location

Category	Types of activity	Key accessibility requirement	Other criteria or policies
A locations City or town centres and major district centres in conurbations	*Regional trip generators* • Office or business centres • Retail centres for specialist or durable goods • Major cultural or leisure attractions • Universities and regional hospitals	• Areas within 800 metres of an intercity rail station • Central in relation to urban public transport	• Low level of car dependence • Parking allowance maximally 25% of theoretical demand • Good pedestrian and bicycle networks linking to nearby residential areas
B locations District centres and centres of small towns	*Town or district generators* • Convenience shopping centres • Leisure centres • District hospitals and technical colleges • Local businesses	• Within 400 metres of an urban public transport node • Embedded within the built-up area • Good pedestrian and bicycling access	• Moderate level of car dependence • Parking allowance maximally 50% of theoretical demand
C locations Edge-of-town industrial estates	*Heavy freight generators* • Regional warehouses • Distribution centres • Manufacturing industry (low employee density)	• Within 2 km of direct access to national road network • Existing or potential access to railways, waterways or coastal shipping	• Road access must avoid residential areas • Area should be accessible by bus or tram
D locations Local or neighbourhood centres	*Local facilities* • Local shops and pubs or cafés • Schools and health centres • Community hall or church	• Excellent pedestrian and bicycling access from the surrounding residential area • Served by a bus or tram route	• Low level of car dependence • Facilities clustered to encourage multi-purpose trips

The requirements and criteria for location suggested here are illustrative and not definitive.

Sources: derived from practice in the Netherlands and adapted from Barton et al. (55)

the traditional role of city, town and district centres. The planning task is to ensure sufficient space and flexibility in land and buildings within these centres to accommodate growth.

Warehousing and extensive manufacturing industry (with relatively few workers per hectare but generating significant freight movement) should be located close to the main road system with potential for good access by rail and waterways or coasts.

Some conventional development patterns are excluded. In particular, low-density single-use estates (office parks, retail parks and campus-style hospitals and universities) in decentralized locations generate huge numbers of vehicle trips while being difficult to access for those without a car. They cause pollution, ill health and social exclusion. Viable alternative forms of development need to be created.

The unit size of facilities

The trend towards an increasing unit size of facilities (notably retailing, schools and hospitals) with extended hinterlands is normally justified by the operators in terms of economies of scale and improved service or choice for users. Nevertheless, it may not be beneficial based on social, environmental or health accounting.

In particular, the investment made in large food stores, large secondary schools and regional hospitals can be directly at the expense of smaller facilities accessible to local communities. Policy providers often ignore the costs their decisions on location and unit size transfer to households – extra use of the car, extra fuel, extra travel time for parents and loss of healthy exercise for children. The commitment of educational institutions, health agencies, recreation managers and others to providing accessible facilities is critical.

HOUSING QUALITY, DIVERSITY AND ACCESSIBILITY

In many city regions there is a tension between the desire to ensure that all households have access to satisfactory housing and the goals of preserving green open spaces and local distinctiveness. Housing is recognized as one of the key determinants of health. Environmental constraints must not be used to justify inadequate housing. Nevertheless, the value of green space for recreation, wildlife, managing water and energy resources and absorbing pollution is great. Within the context of the range of urban form options, the housing strategy can be developed to attempt to achieve both objectives.

The following are useful principles for urban spatial planning.

*   The home is the physical environment in which more than half the urban population spends at least 80% of their time. This figure will rise as more of the population works at home for part or all of the working week.
*   The home should be a private space where people have the space to relax. Overcrowded living conditions and lack of privacy can provoke stress and lead

to mental illness, physical illness and an increase in the accident rate. The mental development of children and young adults is often related to social maladjustment, which can be explicitly linked to poor-quality living conditions.

- Realistic estimates of the total housing needed for the city region over the plan period should be given great weight in decision-making. If supply does not match demand, then price rises force more households to accept poor conditions, living in housing stress or commuting long distances – with severe implications for equity and health.
- Providers of public, social and low-cost housing are central to the interests of the most vulnerable groups. They should be drawn into discussions about a comprehensive housing strategy so that issues of land availability, location and design can be approached coherently. Low-income groups do not gain access to adequate housing simply through ample overall supply but by breaking down the market and institutional barriers both to providing for special needs and the movement of households between sectors (Box 4.3).
- Households need not only adequate housing but also housing in a location convenient to them. Specific housing suppliers will know about this, but a general principle is that every part of the city should have a good range of housing type, tenure, size, price and garden availability. This principle is elaborated in Chapter 5.
- It follows that new housing should not be concentrated in one or two major locations (new suburbs or new settlements) but distributed around the city, allowing households to select a location that minimizes their travel distances and the associated negative health effects *(15,16,59)*.

Box 4.3. Regeneration of social housing and community involvement in Vienna (Austria)

The City of Vienna has defined a series of policies and technical tools for urban renovation and housing restoration through an investigation financed by the United Nations, in which experts from various European countries have taken part. One objective of tenant participation is to minimize the number of tenants who have to move out of their homes. If, following restructuring, the increased rent is higher than a certain percentage of the tenant's income, they are offered a subsidy. The investment to improve housing conditions appears to have psychological importance, especially if combined with tenant involvement. The experience has shown that the tenants involved right at the start of the renovation project are more willing to pay the increased rent.

Source: United Nations Economic Commission for Europe *(60)*

- The variety in housing location is helped by the policy of urban renewal and intensification, which is common to all urban form strategies.
- Density varies tremendously between European cities. Nevertheless, the principle of achieving density consistent with quality safeguards through both renewal and new building is robust. Higher density increases the demand for local facilities and public transport services, facilitates walking and bicycling and reduces the impact on vital resources in open spaces.
- Location and density levels should be determined by accessibility. New housing should not normally be developed on sites that are beyond easy walking distance of a range of local facilities and within striking distance (for example, 5 km) of a major service or employment centre (category A in Table 4.1). Density should be graded, with higher density in the most accessible locations.

Healthy housing does not depend solely on having buildings in appropriate numbers in appropriate places but on an integrated inter-agency approach. Social services, police and health agencies are involved alongside planning, design and engineering services. Box 4.4 summarizes the WHO principles of healthy housing.

Box 4.4.   The WHO principles of healthy housing

Protection against communicable diseases through:
- Safe water supply
- Sanitary disposal of excreta
- Disposal of solid wastes
- Drainage of surface water
- Personal and domestic hygiene
- Safe food preparation
- Structural safeguards

Protection against injuries, poisonings and chronic diseases through attention to:
- Structural features and furnishings
- Indoor air pollution
- Chemical safety
- Use of the home as a workplace

Reduction of psychological and social stress through:
- Adequate living space, privacy and comfort
- Personal and family security
- Access to recreation and community amenities
- Protection against noise

Access to a supportive living environment through provision of:
- Security and emergency services
- Health and social services
- Access to cultural and other amenities

Source: adapted from World Health Organization (61)

INTEGRATING HEALTH, EQUITY AND ENVIRONMENTAL QUALITY IN TRANSPORT PLANNING

The Third Ministerial Conference on Environment and Health was held in London in June 1999 and attended by ministers of environment, health and transport from 54 countries. The Conference noted the potential of integrated strategies to reduce car use while promoting bicycling, walking and public transport (62), and a Charter on Transport, Environment and Health (63) was adopted. This emphasized the key strategic role of land-use policies and urban and regional planning in promoting healthy transport.

Priorities
Every city region needs a healthy transport strategy that coordinates all the modes of transport and is linked to land-use plans to achieve mutual policy reinforcement. The shape of this strategy is widely accepted. It aims to reverse the trend towards dependence on cars. The health priorities for the strategy are:

- to improve air quality, especially in inner urban areas, which often have the highest concentrations of pollution;
- to encourage regular healthy exercise in the form of walking and bicycling, which can increase people's sense of wellbeing and reduce the incidence of obesity, diabetes and heart disease;
- to reduce the level of road traffic accidents, resulting in high levels of death and injury and costs for health care;
- to improve the level of accessibility to jobs and services for those lacking access to a private car, thus increasing their opportunities;
- to enhance the opportunity for social interaction and the development of a sense of community: road traffic can be a significant cause of alienation and isolation in cities, with roads breaking up the community and separating people on two sides of the same street;
- to reduce the consumption of scarce energy and road-building resources; and
- to reduce transport-related CO_2 emissions, which are the most rapidly increasing source of the greenhouse gas emissions responsible for climate change.

Principles

All the main transport agencies in the city region, including national rail agencies and local bus or tram companies, should be involved in preparing and subsequently implementing the strategy. Without their commitment, the strategy is unlikely to work.

Consistency is also critical between different parts of the city region – in inner-city, suburban and rural areas. Car ownership and the level of car dependence vary inversely with density. Paradoxically, the health problems associated with car use are greatest in inner-city areas, where local people use cars least. This has led to very different transport policies in the city and outside. Traffic calming and public transport are supported in town, whereas increased car use continues to be promoted around the city. This schizophrenic approach is completely misguided. Constraints in the city simply push some of the road traffic to the fringes, shifting but not solving problems of pollution and danger. As a result, households and businesses tend to relocate into outlying motor-accessible settlements, potentially threatening the vitality of the urban core. Trips get longer, emissions overall become higher and health is damaged in a number of ways *(15,16,59)*.

Counteracting the growth in transport-related health problems requires concerted action by national governments, the transport industry and local authorities (Box 4.5). The overall strategy includes:

- increasing the cost of motoring by raising fuel prices and charging for road use and parking;
- supporting the healthy modes of walking and cycling and to promote public transport as an alternative to cars;
- developing the land-use pattern and the quality of the environment to encourage walking, cycling and public transport; and
- progressively modifying the engineering of public and private motor vehicles to make them more healthy and safe.

Choice and equity

Constraining car use is often seen as restricting freedom and thus provokes opposition by liberal or market-oriented politicians. However, the arguments can be presented the other way round. The conventional policies that facilitate increased dependence on cars actually reduce freedom. They are systematically disenfranchising those who do not own or do not have use of a car – typically people who are young, old or poor and those most vulnerable to poor health. Even those who use cars contribute to losing their own freedom to walk, bicycle or use public transport because of the collective and individual choices made that increase dependence on cars. So the strategy advocated here is designed to introduce choice for all into the system – to ensure that all population groups can make the trips they need without owning or using a car. The strategy is not so much against cars as promoting health and accessibility. As such, it can have political appeal.

It is not appropriate here to spell out detailed transport policies for city regions. The key policy concepts that should guide policy-making are highlighted. Chapter 5 develops local policies on design in more detail.

Box 4.5.   An integrated approach to managing road traffic in Florence
            (Italy)

To protect the historical centre against traffic congestion, the administration
of the City of Florence launched a wide-reaching project with four main
components:

- improving and extending the suburban railway network to allow greater
  and faster access to the suburbs;
- building up a tram system to connect the suburban car parks with the
  centre, so that people coming from the suburbs can leave their cars and
  transfer to public transport;
- creating special bus lanes: journeys now are faster and more reliable
  and can compete with use of the car; and
- extending the pedestrian area from 25 to 50 ha, with a service of electric
  buses in the historical centre, more bicycle paths and new transport
  technologies, such as the bimodal "scooter" (running on fuel and electric
  power).

Source: WHO Regional Office for Europe *(6)*

Walking and cycling

The WHO pamphlet *Walking and cycling in the city (7)* discusses some of the
health benefits of walking and cycling as well as deterrents, policies and design
solutions.

- A dense network of footways can be created to link all main activities and
  public transport facilities, ensuring safety, directness, ease of use for less mobile
  people and an attractive and secure pedestrian environment.
- Pedestrians should have top priority in the movement system. Where there are
  conflicts with road traffic, the pedestrian routes should be given priority and
  pedestrian route options kept open. This approach was taken in the city of
  Salzburg, Austria, and proved extremely popular with citizens *(2,64)*.
- The level of pedestrianization should be increased where the current or potential
  intensity of pedestrian use justifies it.
- A comprehensive network of convenient cycle routes and a safer cycling
  environment should be developed. This may involve dedicated cycle routes
  (with good visual supervision) especially for school access and recreational
  purposes. More generally, this means slowing traffic on normal roads to a more
  bicycle-friendly speed and making good provision for bicycles at junctions.

Box 4.6.   The ADONIS Project, Copenhagen (Denmark)

The ADONIS Project, Copenhagen, which was funded by the European Union, involved participants from four cities (Amsterdam, Barcelona, Brussels and Copenhagen) investigating ways of promoting cycling and walking in Belgium, Denmark, the Netherlands and Spain to examine different methods of approaching this. It examined best practices in promoting cycling and walking, behavioural factors affecting modal choice, a qualitative analysis of factors increasing cyclist and pedestrian accidents and how to replace short car trips by cycling and walking.

The successful criteria for measures promoting walking or cycling include:

*   making trips attractive and shorter or faster;
*   stimulating walking and/or cycling;
*   being cost effective; and
*   increasing safety (both actual road safety and the feeling of safety).

Important factors in promoting cycling and walking include:

*   setting up an integrated plan and implementing groups of measures step by step, as single measures have limited effects;
*   implementing sufficient crossing facilities for cyclists and pedestrians that allow early detection and good visibility for all road users;
*   increasing the awareness of all road users of each other; and
*   reducing car speeds by traffic-calming measures and/or police enforcement.

The final report *How to substitute short car trips by cycling and walking* is available from the Danish Council of Road Safety Research, Ermelundsvej 101, DK-2820 Gentofte, Denmark, tel: +45 39 680444; fax: +45 39 657362; e-mail: imb@rtf.dk and from European Commission, DG VII/E, Transport Research Help Desk, Avenue de Beaulieu 31, Office 4/83, Brussels, Belgium, tel: +32 2 2954300; fax: +32 2 2954349.

A best practice catalogue *Best practice to promote cycling and walking* giving guidelines for local authorities in choosing key measures is available from the Road Directorate, P.O. Box 1569, DK-1020 Copenhagen K, Denmark, tel: +45 33 933338; fax: +45 33 156335; e-mail: puk@vd.dk.

Sources: Danish Council of Road Safety Research *(65,66)* and Road Directorate *(67)*

Public transport

- The cost-effectiveness of public transport services should be increased. Public transport should have general priority over other road traffic along main routes and to the hearts of areas of high demand (such as city centres), ensuring good interchanges between different services.
- Ticketing systems for different types of public transport should be integrated – for example, local bus, tram and regional train services.
- The aim should be established that all areas of the city and all outlying settlements should be accessible by public transport, not only areas with higher density.
- Thresholds of service quality should be established and used to evaluate current and proposed services and levels of accessibility to residential, business and service areas. Such standards vary according to local traditions and conditions, and appropriate local norms need to be established, based on some research into traveller behaviour. Nevertheless, examples of general guidelines are as follows.
- All new housing should be within 400 metres of a good (or potentially good) bus service.
- All new office, retail and leisure developments should be less than 300 metres of actual walking distance from good public transport services (see also the next section).
- A good service provides realistic competition to cars in availability, speed and price. Service frequency and maximum waiting time should be no more than 10 minutes, with services provided on weekends and evenings as well as weekdays.
- New development should be used to help fund public transport improvements and orient the development towards public transport stops.

Planning of road traffic

- Traditional traffic engineering goals of reducing congestion, improving traffic flows and maximizing capacity and speed need to be replaced by sustainable principles: reduce traffic flow, moderate speeds and restrict capacity.
- New and improved roads should only be approved where essential for ensuring local access and for extending public transport and pedestrian priority.
- Traffic-calmed areas should be extended and the overall capacity for motor vehicles reduced, ensuring a slow but steady pace of vehicular traffic, thus improving conditions for other road users (especially safety). Guideline design speeds:
  - 30 km/h in residential and shopping areas;
  - 50 km/h in other urban zones and main urban roads; and
  - 80 km/h on rural roads.
- Traffic calming should apply equally to suburban areas, rural settlements and city centre or historical areas.

Parking and road-pricing

The common approach to parking is a "predict and provide" policy that supplies spaces to meet expected demand. At the city level, however, restricting parking is the main mechanism currently available for deterring car use. It needs to be carefully devised to reinforce other transport and land-use policies without causing undesirable side effects for residents or preventing car use when this is essential. Policies to control parking must apply equally in suburban and exurban areas and in inner-city areas, to avoid the flight of business from the city and the suburbanization of transport-related health problems.

- The parking provided at all major trip generators (whether in urban, suburban or rural settings) should be kept to the operational minimum as far as possible.
- Standard 10%, 25%, 50% and 75% parking allowances should be applied to business users, depending on the availability of public transport services (see also the policies on location for such users in the next section).
- Temporary permission should be granted for parking where public transport is currently inadequate but planned to improve. When car parking is phased out, the developer can benefit by achieving a higher plot ratio (building density).
- If legislation allows, use other fiscal techniques to reinforce parking control – including taxing private commercial (including shop customer) parking spaces, road-pricing and road tolls.

Park-and-ride schemes

Park and ride may be an appropriate solution:

- in cities wishing to promote a car-free city centre environment;
- in cities with severe traffic congestion and/or restricted central area parking wishing to improve accessibility by attracting travellers to high-quality public transport;
- in cities that attract tourists and wish to protect against the unsightliness generated by large numbers of parked vehicles;
- at large employment sites with restricted car parking, typically as part of a commuter plan initiative; and
- in conservation or historical areas to protect the area people wish to visit where it is desirable to close access roads to all but selected traffic.

Park and ride can be phased in over a number of years, as user awareness and passenger numbers are built up: a step-by-step approach. However, park-and-ride schemes should not normally form part of a long-term sustainable transport strategy except in areas with low density and with poor public transport, as park-and-ride schemes can encourage an increase in car use and in overall travel distances. Recent studies have shown that park-and-ride schemes can encourage an increase in car use and in overall travel distances. Where suburban and edge-of-city park-and-ride services are provided, they attract a significant number of travellers who previously made their whole journey by public transport. This can undermine rural and suburban bus services (except for the primary routes that serve the park-and-ride sites) and increase road traffic in the peripheral city areas. The effect on suburban health and safety is harmful. The overall effect on energy use and CO_2 emissions may balance out, but in some cases is likely to be negative *(68)* (Box 4.7).

• Park-and-ride schemes should only be used in low-density areas where the existing levels of public transport are totally inadequate.
• They should be located as close as possible to the source of travellers – for example, in outlying commuter settlements rather than at the edge of town – and the sites should be designed to encourage patronage by cyclists, walkers and local bus users at least as much as by car users.

RESOURCE PLANNING TO REDUCE THE ECOLOGICAL FOOTPRINT AND IMPROVE HEALTH

Resource management is intimately connected with land-use planning, both because of the profound implications of urban development for resource use and quality and because of the land needed to manage resources. The key resources in focus here are energy, water, food and waste. The health implications of failure to manage resources effectively and the potential health benefits are listed under each resource.

Effective management is difficult in most countries because independent agencies often working at a regional scale take separate decisions. The potential for collaboration to solve intransigent problems or create existing new opportunities is inhibited by conflicts between the agencies' remits and the inertia of established practice. Municipalities have limited power.

Some countries have consciously tried to break down the barriers. New Zealand, for example, has replaced its planning system with a resource management system that attempts to draw together all the resource interests and assesses development proposals based on their effects on resources. In Europe, Sweden and Denmark are probably the most advanced countries in energy-integrated planning. The Netherlands has integrated pollution control with land-use planning.

Fig. 4.4 shows the interdependence of resource and land-use planning.

Integrated resource management
The Healthy Cities approach facilitates the development of collaborative working arrangements between the agencies responsible for different resources (Box 4.8). An early trigger for this could be the production of a joint city health profile (and ongoing monitoring). Opportunities for subsequent joint projects are illustrated by the following examples.

• In Bristol, United Kingdom, an incinerator is burning sewage pellets to generate heat for local industry. The value of sewage in recycling has been recognized

Box 4.7.   The integration of parking and urban policies in Lyon (France)

Lyon is France's second largest city with a population of 1.2 million and is located in southeastern France. It has been confronted with increasing growth of road traffic and congestion problems. SYTRAL (Syndicat Mixte des Transports pour le Rhone et l'Agglomeration Lyonnaise) developed an urban transport plan for the city. This was followed by the construction of a metro and the introduction of a balanced parking control system to improve the environment and improve the general quality of life. This was achieved through a joint public and private venture, the Lyon Park Auto, with the cooperation of a variety of different levels of city and national government.

The strategy for the transport plan included defining a hierarchy of car park supply and eliminating surface car parking, together with extending park-and-ride facilities along peripheral public transport routes. New high-quality underground car parks were located on the core perimeter and in the proximity of major roads to help reduce unnecessary traffic. This allowed for the improvement of public spaces through re-landscaping and incorporating quality design features and works of art. A special feature of the implementation policy is that the public-private company manages the entire system of on-street and off-street parking. The end result is that parking policy has become an urban regulation tool by influencing travel flow and urban land use.

The urban transport plan was adopted in 1990. Although the results have been encouraging, with a satisfactory balance between short-term users, residents and commuters, several further issues need to be refined. These include devising an effective enforcement policy, limiting long-stay parking and finding spaces for the cars of residents of the city centre during the working day in the form of off-street parking. The investment for the programme was FF 700 million over 5 years.

This illustrates how the development of an urban travel plan combining proposals for a metro, a parking control system and extended bus park-and-ride facilities helped to improve environmental quality and public safety. The health benefits of eliminating unnecessary through traffic and improving public spaces can be seen in reduced air pollutants and levels of traffic noise.

Source: EURONET/ICLEI Consortium *(69)*

Fig. 4.4.   Interconnections between resource and development decisions

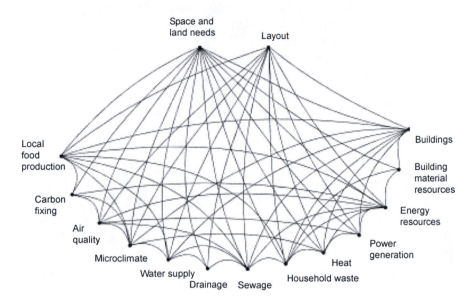

Source: adapted from Barton *(17)*

in two ways. The sewage was previously dried naturally while releasing methane, which heated water to drive an electricity turbine. The ash from the incinerator is converted into compost for farmers. The incinerator can also handle pellets made from organic household waste.

- In Fyn County, Denmark, a farmers' cooperative operates a combined heat and power plant that contributes to the electricity network and supplies district heat locally. The fuel is excess animal slurry. The fly ash from the plant is returned to the land as fertilizer.
- In Kolding, Denmark, an urban renewal scheme has combined housing rehabilitation with high levels of energy efficiency, on-site electricity generation using solar cells and solar hot water. Water is collected from the roof and purified before being used for secondary household purposes. An ambitious on-site wastewater treatment scheme takes the form of a pyramidal greenhouse that provides employment for one of the residents producing fish (for cat food) and flowers for sale from plants, which themselves are helping to purify the water.

All such schemes involve close collaboration between a range of agencies and a supportive legislation regime. They often involve changing regulations or changing patterns that can only be achieved with commitment to a common objective. The urban planners are often key facilitators in the process.

Box 4.8. A strategic plan for the environmental renewal of
            Metropolitan Bilbao (Spain)

Bilbao, the seventh largest city in Spain, is the commercial capital of the
Basque Country. Like many post-industrial cities where heavy manufacturing
was once the predominant sector, Bilbao has suffered a decline since the
1970s, with serious consequences for both the economy and the environment,
and subsequently a loss of inhabitants. The Basque Government, the
Province of Vizkaya and the City of Bilbao attempted to stem this crisis and
to improve the quality of life for the inhabitants of the city by upgrading the
urban environment. These authorities then prepared a strategic plan after a
consensus-building exercise. A nonprofit public-private partnership called
Bilbao Metropoli-30 was established to implement the project. This comprised
more than 100 metropolitan organizations, and the revitalization of the city's
environment and economy was initiated.

The implementation strategy was developed through five phases, with four
main aims:

- progressively reducing the current levels of air pollution;
- fostering plans to renew sewerage and wastewater treatment systems
  to reduce water pollution;
- implementing adequate infrastructure for managing urban solid waste;
  and
- implementing adequate infrastructure for managing industrial waste.

To achieve these aims, a series of strategies was planned that included
developing greater collaboration between universities and private companies,
developing a scheme for environmental auditing, investing in infrastructure
for wastewater treatment, promoting public transport, developing an
environmental database and offering tax incentives for companies to reduce
pollution. The unique feature is the development of such a large independent
partnership with more than 100 members from both the public and private
sectors, voluntary organizations and higher education. Funding has been
over EUR 16 billion from a range of these organizations, and with additional
money from the European Commission.

The results of the strategic plan have led the local inhabitants to reconsider
the benefits of environmental protection and to value the natural environment.
The regeneration projects have improved the quality of both the urban and
natural environments, with a positive outcome for economic prosperity.

Although environmental renewal is a very long-term process, initial progress has already been made together with the development of a system of revitalization indicators by Bilbao Metropoli-30. The scheme demonstrates that the method can be adapted to other major cities with similar problems.

The key health objectives of urban planning highlighted in Chapter 1 identified the importance of good air quality, water and sanitation quality and the need to reduce the contamination of soil by solid waste. This case study illustrates how a long-term strategic plan set about to implement such a project through an independent partnership with positive outcomes for both economic and social welfare and a generally improved quality of life for local residents.

Source: EURONET/ICLEI Consortium *(70)*

Energy strategy

Energy use and the resultant local and global emissions are closely connected to land-use policy in several ways – through the interaction of transport and land use and the level of demand for motor vehicle use, through energy-efficient building policies and through energy supply options.

Every city can have an energy strategy geared to improving energy efficiency and increasing the proportion of energy supply from renewable sources. Sweden and Denmark provide models. Municipalities are given responsibility for coordinating energy supply and use, reducing reliance on nonrenewable sources and improving the quality of life locally. The municipalities are able to manage coordinated programmes of energy efficiency, energy from waste, combined heating and power schemes and district heating.

The potential health benefits of a coherent energy strategy are:

- a reduced incidence of fuel poverty: electricity disconnection, debt, dampness, hypothermia and households living in only one room because they cannot afford to heat the others;
- reduced health-damaging emissions: especially sulfur dioxide, nitrous oxides and other pollutants resulting from the inefficient combustion of wood, coal, oil and natural gas (Box 4.10);
- reduced CO_2 emissions, which will reduce the extent of the greenhouse effect in the long term;
- improvement in health and quality of life of children, especially those in less affluent households, where more household income is used for food and the absence of dampness in the home leads to fewer chills and better school attendance; and
- more local energy-related jobs (especially in insulation programmes) recycles resources locally rather than paying for energy imports, and reduced unemployment brings health benefits.

Box 4.9. An experimental housing energy strategy in Glasgow
           (United Kingdom)

The City of Glasgow (670 000 inhabitants) is the largest real estate owner in
Europe, owning about 140 000 dwellings. One of the biggest problems in
these dwellings is the cost of heating: it is estimated that half the tenants
manage to heat only one room and one quarter cannot afford to heat any
rooms. In the winter months, some young people living alone would have to
spend an estimated 70% of their income on fuel to provide adequate heating.

The municipal authority is firmly convinced that precarious housing means
precarious health since people on low incomes tend to live in poorly insulated
homes and pay the highest energy costs per unit. Glasgow is participating in
the WHO European Healthy Cities network. Based on the principles and
objectives of its work towards becoming a healthy city, Glasgow is carrying
out a study, the results of which will also provide answers to other questions
concerning programmes for improving housing. Hutchesontown is an example
of a specific programme to improve housing within Glasgow.

Hutchesontown is a development of over 1000 homes built in the 1960s
and located 1 mile southeast of the Glasgow city centre. About half the
residents live in four 23-storey tower blocks, together containing 552 one-
and two-bedroom flats; the remainder in four-storey deck-access flats.
Scottish Homes, Scotland's national housing agency, owns and manages
the estate. Like many multi-storey housing developments built around the
1960s, the Hutchesontown development suffered from poor thermal
performance made worse by open balconies, the very exposed position and
off-peak electric storage heating systems that are expensive to run. The
resulting cold and damp conditions led to widespread condensation and
mould-related problems in the homes and considerable discomfort for
residents.

After the area was designated to take part in a special regeneration
programme, a new gas-fired community heating system formed the
centrepiece of its refurbishment. This has been supplemented so that
individual households can control their own system and payment is made
via a card-operated system. The entire block has been overclad with a new
weatherproof skin and windows replaced with double glazing and open
balconies enclosed to form conservatories. Tenant involvement has been a
major feature of the whole operation, from initial survey work through design
and installation work.

The total cost of the heating system refurbishment amounted to £3200 per dwelling. The average heating bills for the new community heating system are estimated to be £3.50 per week (£182 per year), which is a dramatic reduction from charges of up to £700 a year incurred by some residents with the old part-electric heating. The flats are now far more comfortable, and evaluation studies indicate that the scheme has improved the tenants' wellbeing and has alleviated the health problems associated with damp and condensation. From the housing association's viewpoint, the benefits include reduced management and maintenance costs and contributing to reducing CO_2 emissions into the environment.

Sources: Lyon *(71)*, Combined Heat & Power Association *(72)* and Scottish Homes *(73)*

Principles
- Energy should be seen as a key resource, like land, to be managed and allocated by urban policy.
- Energy agencies involved with supply and use, together with consumer interests and social and health agencies concerned about fuel poverty, need to work with the local authority to produce a coordinated strategy.
- The basic aim should be to reduce reliance on fossil fuel while ensuring the availability of adequate warmth and power to the whole population.
- The first priority of development planning is to increase the energy efficiency of buildings, through retrofitting and new building. This has implications for building types – with terraced developments favoured.
- Embodied energy costs can be reduced by using locally obtained low-energy materials and efficient building form.
- Renewable energy can be promoted through design – especially incorporating passive solar features and a layout that ensures good solar access to all buildings (in cooler climates) and adequate summer shade (in warmer climates). Solar water heating and photovoltaic cells are increasingly attractive propositions as well.
- In northern climates, combined heating and power schemes using renewable or low-carbon fuels and supplying district heating networks are viable. They have significant implications for land-use planning in terms of the density of development, mixed use and linearity.

Box 4.10.   WHO guidelines for air quality and energy generation

The WHO guidelines for air quality *(74)* point out that indoor air pollution from using open fires for cooking and heating can cause serious health problems, especially where biomass fuel is burned. An estimated 1.9 million people die annually worldwide from exposure to excessively high concentrations of suspended particulate in the indoor air environment. Indoor pollutants include a wide variety of sources such as tobacco smoke, biological particulate, lead, radon, carbon monoxide and variety of synthetic chemicals.

Strategy for water

Clean water supply and the effective treatment of sewage are fundamental to healthy urban living. Water supply and treatment also use large amounts of energy when they could instead be a source of energy through hydroelectric generation and exploiting the energy value of sewage. Planning controls over development can determine how water is used and abused at each stage of its cycle. Water is also a major user of land.

- A healthy water strategy requires a programme of progressively reducing the unnecessary consumption of pure ("white") water by households and businesses while encouraging the collection and use of rainwater (or "grey" water from washing) on site.
- Industrial and commercial effluent needs to be effectively treated, preferably on site, as does surface water from car parks (where contaminated with oil), so that it can be returned to streams and groundwater uncontaminated.
- All rainwater in built-up areas should be allowed to percolate into the ground (where subsoil permits) to recharge the aquifers on which wells and springs depend and to avoid the danger of flooding. Porous materials for some surfaces are now available. Where run-off is inevitable, then swales and holding ponds can be used.
- Low-energy biological wastewater treatment systems should be progressively introduced (where climate permits) on a localized basis to reduce the use of energy and materials, encourage biodiversity and increase awareness of human ecology.
- Water catchment zones should be safeguarded from inappropriate (polluting) development, flood plains should be safeguarded from any development and streams and rivers should not be canalized, as this exacerbates flooding.

Box 4.11.   Integrated Urban Renewal Project, Kolding (Denmark)

The feasibility of on-site water collection and sewage treatment in inner urban areas has been tested by the Integrated Urban Renewal Project in Kolding, Denmark. The Project involves the rehabilitation of an urban block, located close to the town centre, for 40 homes, 129 flats and 6 businesses, increasing its energy and water self-sufficiency and creating attractive semi-public shared space.

Rainwater is collected on the roofs and passed through a gravel filter before being used for flushing toilets. Wastewater with various levels of contamination is treated in tanks in the inner courtyard and purified in an imposing pyramidal greenhouse using a pond and algae system. A gardener is employed to run this bioworks system, paid from the money saved from reduced water consumption from the public supply and from selling the plants grown in the greenhouse.

The state subsidized the capital cost of the water and wastewater-treatment system on an experimental basis. It is not reproducible in full at the current price of water but does demonstrate the technical feasibility of a high degree of water self-sufficiency in high-density areas. At lower (suburban) densities, other less expensive technologies such as reedbed sewage systems become both possible and cost-effective.

Source: Barton *(17)*

The health benefits comprise security and quality of water supply, avoiding pollution and reducing hazards. A case study for designing a new rainwater drainage system within a new housing development in Denmark helps illustrate some of these points (Box 4.11).

Food

In western Europe, urban and periurban food production has mainly disappeared, with the exception of recreational gardening, although now some health-led community programmes are starting to link nutrition, exercise and local food production. In contrast, local food production and subsistence cultivation is growing in central and eastern Europe and is an important factor for ensuring both food security and supplementing household income. An estimated 10–40% of household income originates from producing and processing homegrown foodstuffs in central and eastern Europe.

An urban food strategy *(19)* could:

- promote food growing in back gardens, allotments and smallholdings;
- encourage composting of organic waste by households and park departments; and
- promote local exchange and sale of food through farmers' markets and local vegetable box schemes.

Urban planners can play a role in this by:

- promoting back gardens that are suitable for food growing;
- safeguarding existing allotments, leisure gardens and productive smallholdings;
- requiring allotment spaces to be provided in all new development, within easy barrow distance of homes (for example, less than 200 metres), or in grouped weekend leisure gardens with essential facilities if high density precludes this;
- incorporating household urban agriculture in green spaces and recreational land uses;
- incorporating gardening areas close to schools and nursery school sites, if not included within them; and
- encouraging farmers' markets in town or district centres.

The potential health benefits could include:

- encouraging healthy regular and hopefully rewarding exercise;
- improving mental health and social inclusion;
- reducing the energy intensity of food production (including chemical fertilizer and tractor use), food processing and transport and improving waste management;
- providing fresher and more nutritious food;
- fostering local employment and commerce; and
- fostering community links.

The Draft Urban Food and Nutrition Action Plan *(19)* produced by the WHO Regional Office for Europe in October 1999 emphasizes the importance of access to safe and healthy food and of developing strategies to improve production methods. Growing the right kinds of foods for health can reduce fuel consumption, pollution, transport and packaging costs and promote biodiversity, especially if food is grown near where it is consumed (Box 4.12). The role of allotments and market gardens is especially significant in achieving these aims.

Box 4.12. Growing vegetables on rooftops in St. Petersburg
(Russian Federation)

People in the Russian Federation have experienced shortages of basic foodstuffs since the early 1990s. Rooftop gardening is considered a novel idea for producing vegetables for urban dwellers who have no access to land outside the city. The potential of rooftop gardening is huge. In just one district in St. Petersburg, 2000 tonnes of vegetables can be grown. St. Petersburg has about 15 rooftop gardens. Shallow bed methods were developed with technical assistance from ECHO (Educational Concerns for Hunger Organization), a nongovernmental organization, with the soil mix being critical for growing plants. Vegetables from rooftop gardens were tested independently for heavy metals and proved to have lower levels of contaminants than vegetables bought and tested from city markets.

Source: WHO Regional Office for Europe *(19)*

Conclusion

The functional interconnections between energy, water, waste and food are profound. When they are considered in a disaggregated way then unsustainable systems evolve. When planned in an integrated way, as in the case study from Kolding, Denmark (Box 4.11), then the potential benefits are immense.

Integrated resource planning is also intimately connected with the system of land use and transport. The pattern of stream and river valleys gives structure to the town. The principle of enhancing local food supply affects the density and pattern of development. Strategic urban planners have to recognize and incorporate these elements rather than simply respond to market pressures for maximum development.

- The creation of partnerships between groups and agencies concerned with economic, social and environmental resources is key to success.
- Coordinated strategies need to be tested against the basic health criteria set out in Chapter 1.

Chapter 5

Neighbourhood planning: counteracting the trend towards placelessness and virtual communities

INTRODUCTION

Neighbourhoods are places where people live. They imply a sense of belonging and of community, with some shared educational, shopping and leisure activities that provide a focus for social life. For many people, especially old and young people and less affluent and less mobile people, the neighbourhood can provide a network of friendships and of mutual support. Such social networks are recognized as being important to happiness and health.

In some cities, especially but not only in the eastern part of the European Region, planned schemes for public housing have created socially uniform, poorly served, inhumane environments where residents have little control over their own situation and problems of poverty, anomie and crime conspire to undermine health. Fostering population stability, community networks and local economic activity in such situations is paramount.

Neighbourhoods are never autonomous and cannot necessarily be separately identified. In older urban areas, they tend to merge into each other, and each individual may perceive a subtly different area as the neighbourhood depending on the location of their dwelling and the main local connections. New suburbs often have clearer edges but fewer local facilities.

The central issue for the planning of neighbourhoods is accessibility by foot. Easy walking distance (for example, 400–800 metres) gives a scale to neighbourhoods. Walking, running, playing and cycling safely in fresh air, meeting people by chance or arrangement and travelling conveniently to places without needing to use a polluting vehicle are key to a healthy community environment. Neighbourhood planning should focus on achieving this.

Reality can be very different. Households have become more private since the middle of the twentieth century; home-based time is increasingly devoted to television and computer; walking, talking and playing on the street have been deterred by noise and danger. At the same time, rising car ownership has reduced the friction of distance, and hence the significance of the locality in people's lives has faded. Interest-based communities supersede place-based communities, large centralized stores replace local shops and neighbourhood services decay for want of a ready market.

Urban policy-makers have often contributed to this decline by a misplaced belief in four principles: land-use zoning, comprehensive development, economies of scale and the inevitability of the motor car. The segregation of land uses, originally conceived to separate dwellings from polluting factories, increases the need to travel to reach employment or services. Comprehensive development of new or old areas can lead to an inflexible physical form and social polarization. Presumed economies of scale lead to the replacement of local schools, hospitals and stores by larger facilities further afield. Supplying roads that can handle high traffic levels facilitates traffic growth with associated noise, fumes, danger, community severance and social exclusion.

Creating healthy neighbourhoods necessarily involves challenging these false principles. Table 5.1 gives an overview of the policies that are needed. The matrix identifies policy objectives for each of the key health issues in relation to the four broad policy areas of housing, local facilities, movement and open space. Little consistency might be expected, given the range of health issues. On the contrary, however, there is a surprising degree of unanimity. A clear neighbourhood planning strategy can be identified:

- increased population stability
- housing diversity and quality
- local jobs
- access to facilities
- pedestrian and cycling networks
- car restraint and public transport support
- a network of open spaces
- a strategy for energy and other resources
- water strategy
- integrated spatial planning
- community development.

The problem is not only to identify a desirable strategy in theory but also to ensure that it is recognized and acted on by the wide range of agencies that need to be involved to make it work: implementing the Healthy Cities approach (Box 5.1). The central concept is one of partnership between public, private and community interests.

PRINCIPLES

Just as a city and its hinterland comprise an ecosystem, so too can a neighbourhood. The basic principles for health and sustainability are similar:

- social: improving the quality of life, especially for less affluent and less mobile people, by increasing local opportunity, choice and convenience, creating a sense of local identity and control and developing community networks; and
- environmental: reducing the ecological footprint of the neighbourhood by minimizing reliance on nonrenewable resources and minimizing the poisoning of the immediate, regional and global environments by pollutants and waste.

Both the social and the environmental objectives stress the importance of localization: of providing locally for local needs. This does not imply that neighbourhoods can become like villages, functioning isolated from their urban context. It means challenging unhealthy trends towards the centralization and globalization of control and instead applying the concept of subsidiarity – returning to or keeping at the local level the opportunities and responsibilities that can most appropriately by fulfilled at that level.

How local is local?

No one neat neighbourhood unit can be defined at the local level. Each person relates to subtly different areas, depending on their individual associations and connections. Different interests and functions can define different neighbourhoods at varying scales. In each case "local" can be determined by reference to the three facets of sustainable development:

- social: the pattern of human behaviour and needs;
- economic: feasible and sustainable solutions at affordable costs; and
- environmental: the severity of effects on resources and ecology.

For example, in relation to primary education, the critical health need is local access for children, so they can be close to home, walk to school and feel like part of the community of young families in an area. If this premise is accepted, it leads to policies on school size and distribution. One study suggests a catchment zone of 600 metres *(55)*.

The catchment areas for most secondary schools are much larger, which matches the larger size of the school. Catchment areas for other activities – such as health centres, local shops, parks and community centres – are likely to vary widely, reflecting patterns of consumer and operator behaviour. What is more, the catchment population necessary to support a given service changes over time. Table 5.2 illustrates the range of catchment populations for local facilities in England. This list is illustrative only and based on experience in England. Catchment areas may vary from place to place and over time. They may be very different in different cultural and institutional settings. Planners should do their own local assessment.

Neighbourhoods in this context are fuzzy concepts. Fixed boundaries are not normally appropriate and may result in insufficient facilities.

Table 5.1. Issues and policy objectives in healthy neighbourhood planning

Key issues	Policy areas			
	Housing	Local facilities	Movement	Open space
Air quality	• Energy-efficient housing stock • Nontoxic materials	• Localize facilities • Locate for pedestrian convenience	• Reduce reliance on cars • Reduce lorry penetration into neighbourhoods and reduce through traffic	• Good microclimate design • Increase tree cover
Exercise	• An attractive, safe residential environment	• Accessible local facilities to encourage walking and cycling	• Convenient and safe pedestrian and cycling routes	• Recreational greenways • Playing fields and playgrounds
Safety	• Design for effective surveillance and clarity of ownership of semi-public and private spaces	• Accessible local facilities to encourage people to be on the street	• Calmed traffic • Design for natural surveillance of footpaths and pavements	• Good visibility across open land
Accessibility	• Develop close to public transport and local services • Grade densities • Prohibit new housing on inaccessible sites	• Localize services within housing areas • Locate for the convenience of pedestrians and access to public transport • Design for disability	• Permeable pedestrian and cycling environment • Plan to ensure that public transport is viable	• Provide accessible open spaces for all kinds of activities
Shelter	• Good range of housing tenure, size and price in every neighbourhood • Energy-efficient housing stock • Siting to reduce heat loss	• Adaptable buildings for local social and commercial uses • Inexpensive to operate and energy efficient • Siting to reduce heat loss	• Bus shelters	• Shelter belts

Key issues	Housing	Local facilities	Movement	Open space
Work	• Support dwelling-based working options • Locate housing accessible by public transport to main work centres	• Foster local small-scale jobs	• Good public transport services to all main centres • A strategic cycling network serving the locality	• Encourage the productive use of open land
Community	• Support community action • Design residential places • Support co-housing and self-build schemes	• Foster local services and employment	• Permeable and attractive pedestrian and cycling environment • Safety on the streets • Design for casual gatherings	• Parks, play areas, playing fields and allotments as meeting places
Water and biodiversity	• Increase water autonomy • Local wastewater treatment and groundwater replenishment • Preserve and enhance habitats	• Increase self-sufficiency in water • Local wastewater treatment and groundwater replenishment • Preserve and enhance habitats	• Ensure local, clean road drainage, replenishing groundwater • Reduce vehicular road traffic	• Structure open space around watercourses to create habitats and conserve water • Create a range of wildlife habitats
Natural resources, soil and minerals	• Build using recycled or renewable materials • Safeguard topsoil • Encourage residential composting	• Build using recycled or renewable materials	• Construct fewer roads	• Facilitate local allotment use and organic recycling • Grow crops that can be used for craft and building materials
Global ecosystem	• Low energy in construction and use	• Low energy in construction and use	• Reduce dependence on fossil fuel	• Grow energy crops • Reduce wind speed by planting • Increase carbon fixing

Box 5.1.   Neighbourhood planning in Horsens (Denmark)

The approach to urban planning in Horsens gives priority to neighbourhood issues throughout the different levels of the process of preparing and implementing plans. The Horsens municipal plan (master plan) *(75)* is one of the few plans to have fully integrated and based its policies on the principles of building a healthy city. The plan, adopted in 1993, combines spatial and strategic planning with citizen involvement. The three main targets of the plan are:

• health promotion – as a basic criteria for all planning activities of the municipal council;
• neighbourhood principles – based on the assumption that creating healthy living environments requires local areas to be administered at a neighbourhood level;
• urban expansion – to create a compact city, with multifunctional zones, without further expanding the residential areas on the outskirts of the city.

In addition to this focus within the municipal plan, the Municipality of Horsens has taken an initiative to prepare urban plans for individual neighbourhoods. This initiative was begun in 1987, with the Gasvej neighbourhood project *(76)*. This project followed Healthy Cities principles, involving the urban planning, environment, social services, education and health sectors and the local community. A plan for the neighbourhood was developed, with residents making suggestions regarding the physical and social environment in order to improve quality of life in the neighbourhood. The process undertaken in developing this plan was as follows:

• analysis of the current situation – including history, social conditions, housing conditions, transport, environment, schools, shops, industry, cultural activities, green spaces and other open spaces;
• examination of existing plans – these included the municipal plan, social services plan, education department plan, development plan, business plan, technological plan and environmental plan;
• use of work groups – groups of residents worked with facilitators to express ideas for the future of the neighbourhood both in writing and using drawings; and
• identification of actions – these were identified as "immediate" and "future".

Although no urban planning activities were identified in the immediate term, those identified for the future included:

- 2–3 community centres with play areas;
- creating more quiet and green streets;
- turning "Lunden" into a public park;
- providing an exchange centre;
- reorganizing the movement of road traffic;
- converting Bredgade into a pedestrian area with trees and other landscaping;
- providing a tunnel under two roads (Strandpromenaden and Sunvej); and
- providing seating areas as part of the streetscape.

The Gasvej project was seen as a first step towards local self-administration. Its success is summed up as follows (76).

> There is a good community spirit in the neighbourhood. We have a proper community centre, which is used for a lot of activities. We meet for group meals every fortnight in the large community centre. There are usually 150–200 people there, and everyone is prepared to lend a hand. We have a lot of events during the year, such as the [Shrovetide carnival]. The whole town talks about how good it is to live in the Gasvej neighbourhood. A lot of new people have moved to the neighbourhood. There are also a lot more children, 200 more than before. We have got a skateboard ramp in Lunden. It was a hard job to get it built. The local authority was not very keen, and afterwards there were a few older residents who could not understand why a skateboard ramp had to be built in that particular place. There are more green areas in the neighbourhood. Whole streets have been turned into quiet residential streets. Café Gasroden has been extended by a barber's shop. There are tables and chairs outside. It is a good place to meet, and hundreds of people visit the café every week. Almost all the residents belong to the residents' association and take an active part in planning the neighbourhood.

Sources: Municipality of Horsens (75,76)

Table 5.2.   Approximate population in catchment areas for local facilities
in England in 1995

Facility	Population in catchment area
Primary school	2 500–4 500
Secondary school	7 000–15 000
Physician's surgery	2 500–3 000
Public house or bar	5 000–7 000
Corner shop	2 000–5 000
Local shopping centre	5 000–10 000
Post office	5 000–10 000
Health centre (four physicians)	9 000–12 000
Library	12 000–30 000
Church or religious centre	9 000 minimum
Community centre	7 000–15 000
Youth club	7 000–11 000
Sports centre	25 000–40 000
Superstore or district centre	25 000–40 000

Source: Barton et al. *(55)*, p. 113

COMMUNITY DECISION-MAKING

Working in partnership

The way local decisions are made is widely recognized as important both in terms of the quality of the decisions and the commitment of local stakeholders to making them work *(26,30)*. The process can also be seen as valuable in itself if it encourages local dialogue and interaction, which reinforces community *(38,55)*. The sense of belonging to an active local community promotes health – especially mental health – by counteracting social isolation and exclusion *(77)*.

While most countries mandate some kind of formal process of public consultation in their planning legislation, the Healthy Cities approach views community involvement as fundamental to a decision-making process that should be shared with the municipality and with business interests. Techniques for structuring involvement at the neighbourhood level include visioning, Planning for Real, focus groups, citizens' juries, stakeholder conferences and environmental fora *(8,38)*. Power can be formally delegated for some purposes to parish and community councils, with action coordinated through decentralized community plans. The two key issues that have to be faced, regardless of the approach, are representativeness and effectiveness. The sections below discuss these issues and then illustrate best practices.

Representativeness and effectiveness

Representativeness is important to ensure that the full range of local views and interests is recognized in the decision process. Such underrepresented groups as

Box 5.2.   Community participation: a charrette process
              in Waitakere (New Zealand)

Waitakere is one of four local authorities in the city of Auckland, New Zealand. It is typified by low-density car-based suburban sprawl and a settler mentality, such that any new development has occurred in the open spaces beyond the city boundary. In 1990 a new Green Party political leadership decided to attempt to redirect development pressures away from the urban periphery (greenfield sites) towards the decaying suburban centres. The council adopted the charrette process (a condensed interactive procedure between all stakeholders over a limited period of time) as a means of engaging all the stakeholders and working for coordinated urban regeneration. The charrette process has been used for each of several intensification zones and involves the following.

- Public debate was triggered and awareness increased through targeted political and professional activity.
- A series of meetings was called with all interested parties – including property owners, retailers, industrialists and community and environmental groups, plus the relevant municipal departments. Some meetings were sectoral but some were explicitly across sectors. People were motivated to attend because of the high-profile public debate.
- The local authority set the broad agenda: urban intensification, community regeneration and priority for pedestrians and public transport.
- Different stakeholders publicly stated their perceived problems, aspirations and ideas for the future, within the framework set by the local authority.
- Working groups facilitated by the local authority devised options that take into account the range of problems and opportunities and that are then debated. If there were apparent conflicts of interest, the relevant stakeholders were involved in searching for a solution.
- The local authority produced a draft master plan, development guidelines and an investment strategy for subsequent consultation.

The outcome of this process was very positive. Attitudes to development were changed, and an effective plan was approved that is now being implemented. The secret was not only the active involvement of the various groups but also the proactive search for solutions that gave everybody clear benefits. The local authority's attitude was critical, combining a non-bureaucratic openness to other stakeholders' viewpoints with a clear vision.

ethnic minorities, unemployed people, poor people and young people are precisely those that experience a higher incidence of ill health and/or accidents. Such groups must be engaged, and any hint of exclusivity (however unintentional) must be avoided.

Inclusiveness is also critical for key decision-makers. For example, in some cases parallel decision-making fora have appeared: one (with power) involving the official agencies and one (without power) raising false expectations among members of the community. The process will only be effective if all the main powerful interests in both the public and private sectors as well as voluntary groups participate fully. An intersectoral approach is required.

Handling such a web of interests is complex. Municipalities have a central role as facilitators. Only they have sufficient leverage on employers, developers, transport operators, water companies, boards of education and the local community to achieve collaboration. The municipality also leads. It should be proactive – setting clear objectives for the process and a framework for decision-making and implementation (Boxes 5.1 and 5.2).

ENSURING SOCIAL INCLUSION AND NEIGHBOURHOOD DIVERSITY IN HOUSING

Principles
Issues of housing availability, choice and quality are normally considered in national and city policies, but they are also important at the level of the neighbourhood. The task for urban planning is to try to match housing availability with housing need in both new and old areas, freeing up the choices open to households.

Every neighbourhood should have a rough balance of different kinds of housing in terms of tenure, size and affordability. The policy appropriate for any particular development area depends on its size and context. Any large development for 2000 or more dwellings should be planned from the outset as a balanced community with the aim of achieving a range of housing types and tenures. To achieve market flexibility, the variation in housing types needs to be applied over the whole area. Some terraced dwellings should be large and others small, and some with gardens and others with just a patio. In this way a proper community balance and social mix can be achieved.

The health objectives should be:

*   to allow households the maximum opportunity to find dwellings that match both their income and their needs, thus reducing housing stress and consequent ill health;
*   to give households – especially transport-disadvantaged people – the chance to select convenient housing locations with good accessibility that minimize the need to travel and cut the level of transport-related pollution;

Box 5.3.   A housing mix in Milton Keynes (United Kingdom)

Milton Keynes is a new city on the main transport lines between London and Birmingham. Its strategic plan involves a net or grid of roads with dispersed residential and commercial activity across it. Each grid square constitutes a neighbourhood of 2000–4000 people with a clear physical identity from which extraneous traffic is excluded. Milton Keynes has pursued a policy of housing diversity within each neighbourhood, successfully achieving a social mix. This has helped to avoid the problems of social exclusion and enabled households to find suitable accommodation in any part of the city, reducing the average length of journeys.

The diagram illustrates how each neighbourhood is divided into a patchwork of home zones, each one developed by a different agency, house-builder or self-builders. Housing for rent, housing with shared ownership and a lower price and housing with a higher price each account for about one third of every neighbourhood.

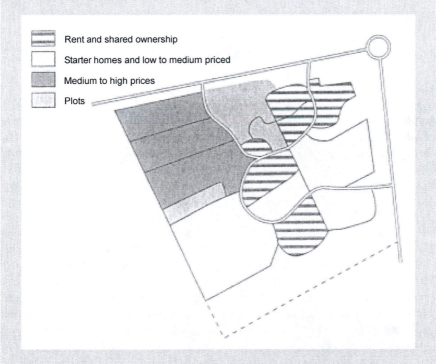

Source: Barton et al. *(17)* adapted from Milton Keynes Development Corporation *(78)*

- to avoid peaks and troughs of demand for local facilities (especially in relation to children, adolescents and older people), which lead to insufficient or excess supply; and
- to reduce problems of social exclusion and isolation and to foster a sense of community.

Implementation

Identifying local housing needs that are not adequately met requires the municipality to consult with the local community and housing providers. It also means going against the common presumption of more of the same. Instead, diversity is the essence. Where a neighbourhood comprises only expensive private housing, affordable public or social housing is needed (and vice versa). Where detached housing predominates, then more apartments may be appropriate (Box 5.3).

The policy should apply to both new and old zones. In some areas it may mean confronting the presumptions of the market to ensure that the most vulnerable groups have options open to them. In this situation implementation may require stronger manipulation of the market than simple planning policy can achieve. In the Netherlands, for example, municipalities buy and own new housing land. In England, the owner of any development over 30 units can be obliged by legal agreement to provide some low-cost dwellings.

PROMOTING ACCESS TO LOCAL FACILITIES

Principles

A good relationship between housing and local employment, retail, education and health facilities is critical to establishing healthy neighbourhoods. It means that people without access to a car can get local jobs and use neighbourhood shops, clubs, school and health facilities. In addition, it means that a higher proportion of trips will be on foot or bike, and even those who do use cars will not have to travel so far. Casual meetings between people increase and facilitate friendship networks and a sense of community.

The difficulty is that rising car use and falling urban density have reduced the attractiveness and viability of local services in many cities. These unhealthy trends have often been promoted by planners by misplaced emphasis on free-flowing traffic, land-use zoning and ambitious development schemes that sideline localities. The positive alternatives are calmed traffic, mixed use and small-scale development.

Localities should be planned so as to foster the viability of local jobs and facilities, by ensuring good access by foot and bicycle and by encouraging the clustering of facilities in ways that can adapt and flourish as social and market conditions change (Fig. 5.1).

Fig. 5.1.   Towards healthy policies

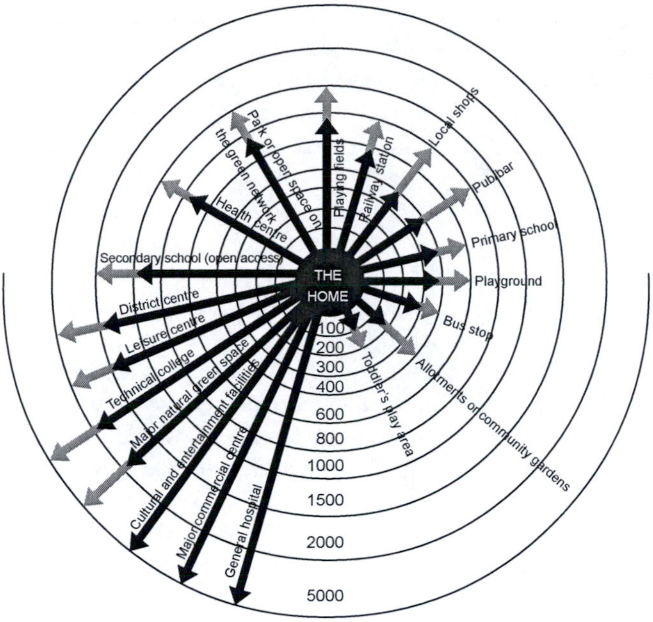

Source: Barton et al. *(55)*

Health objectives in relation to planning local facilities include the following.

- A good range of local job opportunities increases options, especially for the groups – such as people with few marketable skills, less mobile people, single parents and young people – that are vulnerable to health problems associated with poverty and unemployment.
- Access to services is a key factor in promoting health and helps combat the inequity experienced by people without cars.
- Increasing the number of walking and cycling trips is good for health.
- Reducing the necessity of car use allows policies to be put in place that restrain and calm traffic and cut emissions. This encourages local facilities by making streets pleasanter and safer, thus contributing to both health and wellbeing.
- More people on the streets and at facilities fosters local community and creates a safer environment for children.

All new buildings should be accessible to a full range of facilities to minimize journey length, facilitate walking and cycling and increase accessibility. Appropriate access standards should be incorporated into the development plan and into subsequent design briefs.

Implementation

Urban planners need to work closely with the private, public and voluntary sectors in locating facilities. Businesses have specific requirements for location that are often not fulfilled by traditional neighbourhood design. Shops, for example, require high pedestrian density, flexible catchment areas and good visibility. The public sector often has development programmes that centralize rather than localize (local hospitals closed in favour of city-wide hospitals) and may need changed remits to encourage them to think locally. The voluntary sector often has distinctive projects, unique to an area, that can help reinforce a sense of local ownership.

Implementation can be greatly helped if planners achieve clarity of purpose and define the criteria to be used in making policies. The lessons of the past, however, in which the planning of neighbourhoods has sometimes run counter to human behaviour, suggest caution. Traditional approaches to local facilities, as in many towns and suburbs that were developed in the twentieth century, equated facility catchment areas with discrete, bounded neighbourhoods (where through movement is excluded). The problem with this approach is its inflexibility, as it cannot recognize different sizes of catchment areas or adapt to changing economic conditions, social preferences and population patterns. It also offers limited choice to residents in any particular neighbourhood. Facilities in such discrete locations may wither as consumers demand more choice and have higher mobility.

For these reasons, neighbourhood planning should avoid falsely deterministic models, with fixed catchment areas and impermeable boundaries. Instead, neighbourhoods should be seen as part of an urban continuum, one melting into another, with free pedestrian and cyclist movement through them, and facilities that can find their own catchment area.

Towards healthy policies

The following are general guidelines for the spatial planning of local facilities. They are generic and not specific because the urban contexts across Europe vary widely, along with service thresholds and standards of access.

- Encourage the localization of health, education, social and retail facilities.
- Cluster facilities, including employment providers, along local high streets and in town centres, to encourage multi-purpose trips.
- Ensure that catchment populations and areas can vary according to the needs of different activities now and as they may change in the future.
- Grade housing density so it is higher near the facility clusters and lower when further away, and apply this grading to renewal as well as greenfield schemes.
- Identify desirable thresholds of accessibility for key local facilities and plan accordingly – for example, a junior school should be within 800 metres of every household.
- Ensure ease of movement (on foot) between housing areas, and do not define neighbourhoods with fixed boundaries.

- Encourage (or sustain) local workshop and office spaces, mixed in with the housing, and apply a strict maximum size and parking limit to avoid the dispersal of major employers into residential areas.
- Establish strict good-neighbour principles in relation to noise, fumes and access to light.

PLANNING FOR MOVEMENT

Principles

The aim of transport is to get to places, normally (it is assumed) by vehicular means. Movement, on the other hand, implies that there can also be value in the moving itself, and the means may simply be bodily activity.

The health objectives of planning for movement locally are therefore:

- encouraging healthier lifestyles – more walking and cycling;
- reducing accidents on the street;
- reducing the fear of assault and street crime;
- improving access to local facilities and to public transport services, especially for transport-disadvantaged people and less mobile people;
- creating streets and places where people can meet and thus foster local networks of support, improving quality of life and fostering a sense of community; and
- reducing traffic-related air pollution and CO_2.

Key to all these objectives is getting people from all sectors of society to walk. Research shows that people's propensity to walk is very significantly affected by how safe, convenient and pleasurable the experience of walking is. Safety is also a key factor in encouraging cycling, especially for children and older people. Public transport use is profoundly affected by distance to stops, reliability and the speed and comfort of service as well as frequency. Achieving these objectives requires close cooperation with transport providers and effective land-use planning.

Planning for the pedestrian

Walking is the most common form of movement, open to almost everybody. It constitutes most trips for people who do not own a car, especially women and children *(79)*. Like cycling, walking involves minimal resources but can be a healthy and pleasurable aesthetic and physical experience. Yet the pedestrian environment in many cities is increasingly hostile, and this is being exacerbated by the car-oriented nature of much modern development. In extreme cases the pedestrian option is being effectively excluded by inconvenience, danger, fumes and ugliness.

The following are policies for promoting walking.

- Every development, large or small, should have direct, convenient and visible access for pedestrians. Shops, pubs and health centres, for example, can front the street or square rather than giving access across their car park.
- The pattern of footpaths and pavements should allow good permeability – a choice of routes filtering through an area and giving convenient routes from anywhere to anywhere.
- Facilities should be clustered to provide extra incentive to walk to them, with housing located within easy walking distance.
- No new housing should be permitted on isolated sites (beyond set distance thresholds) unless it is built at a scale to generate new local facilities.
- Safety from road traffic should be provided by effective calming techniques and not normally by grade separation or fences that restrict pedestrian freedom.
- The detailed design of all pedestrian routes needs to attend to directness (reducing distances to facilities and neighbourhoods) and convenience (avoiding steep hills, steps and kerbs that might inhibit physically less mobile people and people who use wheelchairs and pushchairs (strollers)).
- Key to the pleasure and potential social benefits of walking is getting to places where it is natural to stop and look, meet people and sit down. In cities such places can be squares, pocket parks or simply broader pavements by shops, cafés or bus stops.

Planning for the cyclist

Cycling provides excellent exercise and improves accessibility. According to research in the United Kingdom *(55)*, the average cycling journey is 3 km, with a threshold of about 5 km beyond which bicycles are generally not used. The propensity to cycle is strongly affected by the safety and convenience of routes available. The cycling habit is best forged when young, so creating safe routes to schools, parks, local shops and around residential neighbourhoods by working with parents, teachers and children themselves is a priority. The healthy planning challenge is to increase the amount of cycling while reducing accidents to cyclists. This is particularly difficult because cycling is a relatively anarchistic activity that is not easily regulated. Indeed, the freedom of cycling, the ability to go from anywhere to anywhere, is one of its attractions, with probable psychological benefits.

The criteria for designing cycle networks include access, safety, continuity, directness, comfort and cycle racks or other parking.

Access. General-purpose streets, which give direct access to homes and facilities, need to be bicycle friendly, with traffic calmed. Segregated routes are desirable in some situations (such as greenways through parks) but are no substitute for roads on which people can cycle safely.

Safety. Separate lanes or paths can be provided if conflict with heavy or fast-moving traffic is unavoidable. Eighty percent of accidents are at or near junctions, where cars turn across cyclists' path. Measures to give bicycles priority at junctions are therefore especially important.

Continuity. Main bicycle routes should be as continuous as possible, with few stops. Fragmented stretches of bicycle path can actually increase overall dangers, so the process of implementation should allow for safe intermediate stages.

Directness. Cyclists do not normally accept diversions that increase their journey length, time or effort significantly (for example, by more than 10%). Segregated routes are sometimes impractical since the direct route in existing urban areas is via the main road. In new development, priorities can be reversed, giving the most convenient route to cyclists and pedestrians.

Comfort. Special cycling routes need to be very carefully designed in detail, and subsequently maintained, to ensure easy gradients (normal maximum 5%), a smooth surface, protection from the fumes from and intimidation by heavy goods vehicles and a visually attractive experience.

Bicycle parking. Secure end-of-journey parking in convenient locations is a factor affecting bicycle use – for example, at railway stations. Encouraging bike and ride effectively extends the catchment area of the station.

Public transport operation
The pattern of bus services in a neighbourhood is too important to be left to the operators. The planners can significantly affect the viability of public transport and the route network in new areas by arranging roads, footways and land uses. The quality of bus and train service can be higher where the maximum number of people can reach their destination by the minimum number of routes. Linearity is therefore a key feature. The points where routes cross (nodes) then become the prime locations for local jobs and services and the focus for pedestrian and cycling routes. Public transport accessibility needs to be considered not therefore as an afterthought (left to the market) but as the starting-point for neighbourhood planning, with land uses then attached to the public transport network (Fig. 5.2).

Access to stops and stations
Ideally, all housing development should be within easy walking distance of good public transport services that give access to the main centres of urban activity (Box 5.4). A common standard for bus access across Europe is 400 metres. Beyond that distance, the proportion of people willing to walk declines progressively and car dependence increases. The 400-metre criterion needs to be applied with care. It is the distance people actually walk; if routes are indirect, the straight-line distance

Fig. 5.2.   Principles of public transport planning

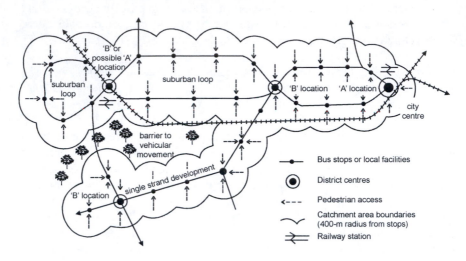

Source: Barton et al. *(55)*, p. 124

may be much less. Access is also influenced by gradients (especially for older people) and psychological barriers such as subways or intimidation by road traffic. Conversely, most people are prepared to walk further for high-quality metro or tram services.

Planning road traffic

The key to a healthy transport strategy is taming vehicular traffic. The capacity of the road system should not normally be increased, because it simply encourages extra trips by car and compounds problems of air pollution and (sometimes) accidents, undermining the inclination to walk, cycle or use the bus. On the contrary, road capacity may be progressively reduced (allowing time for behavioural adjustment) as a direct consequence of positive planning for other modes of transport, such as:

*   widening pavements and safeguarding pedestrian safety;
*   inserting special bike lanes and measures to give cyclists priority at junctions; and
*   creating bus-only lanes and tramlines.

Road traffic speeds

Since the speed of traffic is a prime factor in accidents, appropriate speed limits need to be built into the design of roads and of traffic management measures. The standard design speed in residential areas and shopping streets should be about 30 km/h. This can be achieved by narrowing road widths, making tight bends, reducing sightlines and installing junction platforms and rough surfaces (making a smooth path for bicycles). Road humps (bumps) should not normally be used. They are awkward for buses and cause extra pollution and noise as vehicles brake and accelerate. The objective should be slow but constant traffic speed.

PUBLIC SPACES AND OPEN SPACE

Principles

Wild places, green parks, smaller squares and other community spaces are all important. In many cities, open space is controlled by a variety of interests: a football club's playing field, a municipal park, a farm pasture on the flood plain. If healthy and sustainable environments are to be achieved, this single-purpose, uncoordinated approach is inadequate. Open space has many overlapping functions relating to both human activity and the physical environment. These functions have to be recognized, and the various agencies need to work in harmony to achieve a healthy urban environment. Far from being the residual gaps left over after development has occurred, open spaces require a coherent multi-agency strategy.

Public open spaces play an essential role in safeguarding and promoting the health of the community (5). Individuals must be able to relax in contact with the elements of nature in green spaces in numerous ways: recreation, social, cultural and physical activities. The survey of urban planners in cities participating in the WHO European Healthy Cities network (51) suggests that the accessibility of green space varies enormously in different countries, but one measure that can be used as a fundamental criteria for checking on the availability of space is to consider the distance away from the homes of the users. In Brussels, Copenhagen and Glasgow, all residents can reach a green space in 15 minutes. In many cities the percentage is far lower: for example in Bratislava and Kiev only 47% could do so.

The open space strategy needs to work towards an urban green network accessible to all residents and structured around water and woodland to let the city breathe. This should be complemented by a network of squares and other outdoor facilities throughout the city.

The overlapping functions, related to health, wellbeing and quality of life are water management, absorbing pollution, climate modification, recreation, urban food and fuel production, CO_2 sequestration and wildlife habitats.

Water management. The management of water includes surface water drainage, treatment of grey (slightly polluted) and black (extremely polluted) wastewater and controlling flooding.

Absorbing pollution. Vegetation, especially trees, breaks up and counteracts the concentration of pollution in cities, freshening the air.

Box 5.4. A car-free development in Edinburgh (United Kingdom)

Restricting the freedom to own a car is often seen as politically unacceptable. But the Edinburgh car-free housing development has uncovered a surprising level of pent-up demand from potential residents wanting freedom from the danger and health hazards of the car. The scheme for 120 flats is being constructed where local facilities are easily accessible by foot and public transport connections are excellent. The density of the scheme can be high because space is not wasted in providing residents car parking. The four-storey blocks (based on traditional Edinburgh tenements) surround a generous shared garden and are accessed by a pedestrian street and cycle route.

The buildings are designed to maximize solar gain and have very good levels of energy efficiency, minimizing space heating requirements. Thus, fuel poverty and the consequent health problems common in public housing in the United Kingdom will be eradicated here. The building materials are maintenance-free and recyclable and are chosen for minimum environmental impact.

The project was initiated by the City of Edinburgh's Planning Department and is being developed by the Canmore Housing Association and Malcolm Homes Ltd. Considerable legal hurdles have been overcome to try to ensure that the development and the surrounding area remains car-free. It is too early to determine whether the car-free ruling can be enforced in practice once people have bought or rented their dwellings.

Source: Kleiner *(80)*

Climate modification. At the city level and locally, excessive summer heat and winter cold are moderated by planting trees and ensuring green spaces. Where appropriate, banks of trees can be designed as shelter belts, reducing the heat loss from buildings.

Recreation. Green spaces within striking distance of homes provide the setting for healthy exercise and an inducement to walk and cycle for pleasure. Hard landscaped squares can provide recreational and leisure facilities for all ages, including basketball courts, football fields, cafés, outdoor music and theatre venues and other meeting places, which all contribute to the quality of life.

Urban food and fuel production. Allotments, leisure gardens and horticulture can increase local food production, with potential benefits in improving food quality, ensuring recycling of materials and reduced packaging, reducing the use of fossil fuels and contributing to biodiversity. They can also provide opportunities for healthy exercise, community development and social inclusion.

CO_2 sequestration. Increased tree growth can help fix carbon and thereby compensate for some of the high urban CO_2 emissions and reduce the ecological footprint of the city.

Wildlife habitats. The wildlife habitats in cities benefit human wellbeing and the quality of life as much in terms of education and as a community resource as they benefit wildlife.

Implementation
Ownership and access, rights of access and protecting privately owned space are all important. Planning can also help to create new public open spaces such as squares, pocket parks and playgrounds at appropriate locations by ensuring that strong standards in terms of levels of services and accessibility are implemented. This can be done both through renewal and regeneration schemes in older urban areas and through the regulatory planning process in new developments.

CONCLUSIONS

An experimental approach
Cultural norms vary widely between cities and countries. A solution that works in one city may not in another. Adopting a systematic and experimental approach to implementing policy is important.

The essence of the experimental approach is open-mindedness. Fig. 5.3 provides an example applied to employment policy. It shows the wide range of potential benefits as well as problems. The skill of the planner, in collaboration with economic development specialists and the private sector, is to devise a detailed policy that will maximize the benefits while minimizing the problems. This requires a creative and flexible approach. Bureaucratic reliance on past policy conventions will not do. In addition, while implementation is occurring, monitoring the effectiveness of the policy is essential. Is it being implemented as intended? If not, why not? Is it having the predicted outcomes? Are there any unanticipated side effects? The planner must then adapt, weave and cajole to make it work. The policy is an experiment being tested in the real world. Like any experiment, it may go wrong.

Fig. 5.3.   Neighbourhood policy analysis: local employment

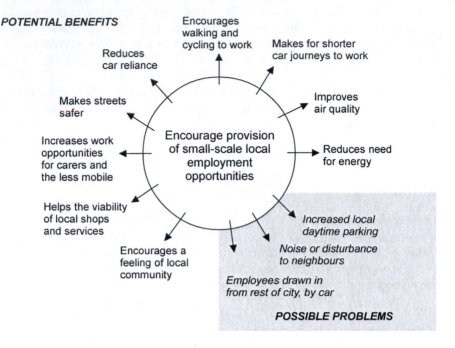

POTENTIAL BENEFITS

Encourages walking and cycling to work

Makes for shorter car journeys to work

Reduces car reliance

Makes streets safer

Improves air quality

Increases work opportunities for carers and the less mobile

Encourage provision of small-scale local employment opportunities

Reduces need for energy

Helps the viability of local shops and services

Increased local daytime parking

Encourages a feeling of local community

Noise or disturbance to neighbours

Employees drawn in from rest of city, by car

POSSIBLE PROBLEMS

Evaluation

Another vital process is evaluating the overall scope and content of plans as they are being devised by referring to the original objectives. Box 5.5 illustrates how one goal can be used to derive a range of possible policies. How far has the plan incorporated them?

Box 5.5. Relating health objectives to neighbourhood policies:
an example

Objective 1: healthy air quality

The following are possible policies.

Housing
• Improve the energy efficiency of the housing stock
• Build using nontoxic materials
• Increase housing density near local facilities and public
  transport services
• Refuse to allow new housing in inconvenient locations

Facilities
• Increase local job opportunities
• Deter polluting industry
• Encourage local schools, shops and leisure facilities
• Deter employers and facilities with a city-wide catchment area

Open space
• Develop a local network of open spaces
• Increase tree planting
• Design for a good microclimate

Movement
• Plan convenient, safe and attractive pedestrian and cycling routes
• Improve access to public transport
• Reduce lorry penetration into the neighbourhood

Source: adapted from Barton *(17)*

Chapter 6

Assessing a project

INTRODUCTION

This chapter develops the principles of healthy urban planning at the level of the specific site or project – for example, a mixed-use renewal scheme, a new retail outlet or a new housing development. The range of issues will encompass not only those dealt with in earlier chapters (acting as a project level summary) but also matters specifically relevant to site appraisal and design evaluation.

The format is a checklist of questions intended to assist the people making decisions about developments, including project managers, designers, development control officers and people working on detailed local plans, in assessing the extent to which a specific project, or alternative development options, fulfils health and sustainability criteria. The checklist is indicative rather than comprehensive. The first section works through the process of consultation and establishing partnerships with relevant agencies and the local community. The subsequent sections address the key substantive issues of need, location, context, site appraisal, design and layout and building quality.

The checklist is approached from the viewpoint of the municipal planning department but is equally relevant to the socially responsible developer and to community interests. The idea of the checklist derives from several sources. At a general level, it is linked to established processes of environmental impact assessment. Some countries and municipalities are extending the environmental impact assessment principle from large projects where it is obligatory to all development projects, at the same time extending the scope to embrace social and economic as well as environmental criteria more fully. This project assessment could therefore be called brief health impact assessment or sustainability impact assessment. Much of the detail in the checklist is based on a guide to the planning of sustainable settlements *(55)* in the United Kingdom. Nevertheless, the ideas and approach are appropriate throughout Europe.

There are four sources of development initiatives:

• the landowner – who wishes to gain a permit on a specific site or to influence a detailed local plan for an area in order to sell land;

- the developer – who wishes to build houses, offices or factories for sale or lease and identifies sites where this might be profitable;
- the municipality – in the role of landowner and/or developer; as municipalities often own substantial land, they need to identify the most appropriate sites for development; and
- the end-users – who wish to find or build accommodation for their own use.

For clarity, the checklist takes the starting-point of the development project rather than a specific site. It also assumes that there are factors related to both housing and commerce. Users of the checklist have to decide which questions are relevant to their situation.

THE PROCESS OF DECISION-MAKING

Consultation is a necessary part of the decision-making process even for house-holder development proposals, but larger projects must often go beyond consultation if a coordinated and healthy scheme is to result. Other interests will be at stake. Action by a range of agencies (such as infrastructure agencies and service providers) is likely to be critical to the quality of the outcome.

Establishing the need for the project
- Is an end-user already involved?
- Is the project responding to needs identified in the development plan or master plan for the area?
- Is there backing from the wider community for the principle of such a project?
- Is the project tied to the site by reason of the project's specific characteristics, or is the project footloose?
- Do relevant infrastructure and service agencies agree that the particular site should be developed?

Working with the relevant agencies
- Is there a clear framework agreement at the outset between the project developer and the local planning authority that establishes who should be partners or consulted in the decision process and how they should be involved, given the particular scale and nature of the project?
- Are the specific project development interests appropriately involved:
  - landowners?
  - developers?
  - any current tenants in or owners of the site?
  - potential end users?

- Are relevant infrastructure providers involved:
  - providers of transport infrastructure?
  - operators of public transport?
  - agencies for water supply, sewage treatment and drainage?
  - companies providing gas, electricity and district heating?
  - education, leisure, health, police and fire services?
- Is the community actively involved:
  - neighbours?
  - local neighbourhood groups?
  - urban social, environmental, civic and economic lobbies?

Mechanisms for cooperation
- Has an effective working partnership been established between all key stakeholders, with a cooperative attitude established so that issues and possible solutions can be properly recognized and evaluated?
- Are community interests being effectively recognized through public meetings, focus groups, Planning for Real, citizens' juries or other appropriate means, on a practical time scale and with participation of the key players, so that the results can be properly incorporated in the development proposals?
- Is the professional and technical work being staged in such a way that decisions are not reached prematurely and the health, social, environmental and economic context of the project and the site is fully taken into account?
- More particularly, does the project programme include the following stages:
  - site, context and stakeholder assessment?
  - based on the assessment, preparing a development brief and master plan or site plan?
  - in the context of a validated brief and master plan, a detailed design and construction programme?
  - in the wake of construction, user involvement in on-going management and monitoring to ensure that the objectives are achieved?

CHOOSING THE RIGHT LOCATION

This section examines whether a given site is appropriate for development. The checklist could also be used to compare and evaluate alternative sites. The main health issues raised relate to the quality of the environment, safeguarding resource quality and the level of accessibility.

A site can be assessed in respect of each of the questions below using the following choices:

- critical constraint: the problems are so serious as to normally preclude development;

- transferable constraint: the problems are serious but might be solved by collaboration off site;
- negotiable constraint: the problems can be solved by good design on site;
- neutral: the question has marginal or no relevance;
- opportunity: development can help solve on-site problems; and
- priority: development can help solve wider problems and create quality.

Pollution and hazards
- Is the site, or part of the site, subject to excessive levels of air pollution, noise, vibration, ground contamination or industrial hazard, beyond what can be solved by good design?
- Is the development liable to cause excessive levels of pollution, noise or danger for people in the vicinity, either directly through the nature of its activity or indirectly because of traffic generated? This applies most obviously to industrial or extractive activities in residential areas.

Water resources
- Does the proposed site avoid areas susceptible to flooding and avoid exacerbating problems of excessive surface run-off?
- Is it located where there is spare capacity in the water supply system (or on-site catchment potential), avoiding areas where groundwater abstraction rates are not sustainable?
- Is it located where there is spare capacity in the surface and wastewater drainage systems or on-site potential to deal with these?

Minerals, land and soil
- Does it avoid high-grade soils, areas with organic farming and with intensive local food production (such as allotments)?
- Does it safeguard potentially usable virgin or recyclable mineral resources?
- Does it reuse or reclaim derelict urban land and thus reduce pressure on greenfield sites?

Energy use
- Is the site in a sheltered position, avoiding exposed hill crests?
- In cooler climates: is the site level or gently sloping towards the sun, avoiding north-facing zones, to maximize the potential for solar gain?
- In cooler climates: is the site in a position to benefit from the introduction of district heating and combined heating and power in the wider area or to help justify the extension to the network that would benefit others?
- In warmer climates: is the site able to take advantage of shelter belts and planting for shade? Are there adequate groundwater supplies and reserves available?

Biodiversity and carbon fixing

*   Would development on the site affect a protected wildlife conservation area or valuable wildlife habitat?
*   Will the development conserve and potentially enhance woods and copses?

Movement networks

*   Is the site well served by existing or potential walking and cycling routes that offer safe and convenient routes to local facilities and by public transport services?
*   Could the development of the site help to justify the improvement of public transport services? Could it contribute financially?
*   Is there reasonable road access to the site without exceeding the physical capacity of the road network or causing environmental damage or increased danger?

Accessibility

*   Would potential residents have good access to a wide range of jobs both locally and regionally without being obliged to rely on using a car?
*   Would residents be within easy walking or cycling distance of a good range of local facilities – social, health, leisure, shopping, education and open space?
*   Would commercial users be embedded within an urban area so that a good proportion of employees or clients are within walking or cycling distance?
*   Would the development help to reinforce the viability and vitality of local service centres by increasing their catchment population and/or by complementary commercial or social activities?
*   Do employment or social facilities have an appropriate degree of accessibility by public transport to afford easy access from the surrounding area to:
    *   local facilities on a main local bus or tram route?
    *   district facilities at a nodal point for local public transport services?
    *   city-wide facilities at the hub of services, including close to main-line rail services?

The built environment

*   Could the site potentially provide an attractive environment for people living, working and playing: safe streets, pure air, pleasing aesthetics (sound, site, smell and touch)?
*   Would it have the capacity to enhance the environmental quality of the neighbourhood, preserving what is valued, including history, townscape and landscape, while regenerating dead, hazardous or ugly elements?
*   Would development enable existing structures on site to be rehabilitated or, failing that, their materials reused?

SITE ASSESSMENT

Good analysis of the site and its context are necessary if the principles of healthy planning are to be converted into practice in the development or renewal scheme. It is critical that developers (and their designers) engage in this assessment and understand its significance. To encourage this, the municipality could oblige developers to submit a site assessment in support of their development application. Such a submission could take the form of annotated maps and a short statement of stakeholder consultations.

From the health and sustainability viewpoint, the following questions are important.

Ground conditions and topography
- Has the condition of the soil and ground been investigated to determine stability and bearing capacity?
- Are there past (potential) mineral workings or areas of landfill on or adjacent to the site that might cause hazard?
- Is the ground contaminated with any hazardous materials, and have radon levels been checked?
- Have slopes been analysed in terms of gradient and aspect to guide design decisions so as to:
  - minimize cut and fill and retaining walls?
  - minimize disruption of natural drainage?
  - maximize solar gain or shade (according to climate)?
  - avoid undue exposure?

Microclimate, air and noise
- Have the implications of prevailing insulation levels, wind patterns, diurnal air flows and frost risk been considered?
- Have sheltered positions been identified, especially in relation to neighbouring buildings and tree shelter belts?
- Is the site affected by sources of pollution or noise, especially major roads or factories?
- Is there potential on site or by agreement with neighbours for mitigating or reducing levels of pollution or noise?

Water and wildlife and landscape
- Has the amount and quality of rainwater and its potential for use on site been assessed?
- Has information been gathered on infiltration, groundwater and watercourses (flow, pollution and wildlife interest)?
- Has the potential for on-site treatment of grey and black wastewater been evaluated?

- Is there potential for treatment of polluted watercourses to enhance on-site health and biodiversity?
- Has a wildlife survey been conducted, identifying habitats (often associated with watercourses) that are inherently valuable and could contribute distinctive character to development?
- Have locally significant landscape features been identified (on or near the site) such as tree groups, streams or crests of hills?
- Does the site contribute (now or potentially) to a green corridor important for recreation, wildlife or the landscape?

Reuse of buildings and local materials
- Have existing unused or derelict buildings on the site been assessed for their historic or townscape value and the viability of retaining them?
- If demolition is unavoidable, is there potential for reusing the materials?
- If buildings or plots within the project area still have tenants (often with low ability to pay rent), what potential is there for retaining or improving these buildings?

Movement and accessibility
- What existing or proposed pedestrian or cycling routes, desire lines (routes people instinctively take through an open space) and rights of way could be affected (positively or negatively) by the project?
- Where are the nearest bus, tram or rail stops, and how could access be gained most directly and safely to them from the site?
- Where are the nearest schools, surgeries, shops, cafés, bars, children's play areas, parks and playing fields in relation to the site?
- How does the time or distance to these facilities compare with approved standards (see Table 4.1 for suggested distances)?
- Do existing or possible pedestrian and cycling routes offer good quality in terms of:
  - road traffic safety?
  - gradients and surface?
  - ease of use by people who are less mobile?
  - attractiveness?
  - directness?
- Do any specific new links need to be made to avoid a land-locked site and improve permeability?
- Are the relative merits of different possible vehicle access points identified in terms of noise and danger (on and off site) and ensuring a permeable road network?

Land use and character
- What are the surrounding uses? Is there potential complementarity with proposed uses on the site, especially in terms of pedestrian movement?
- Can development on the site be used to trigger renewal or revitalization on neighbouring sites (thus enhancing the land values of both)?
- What is the prevailing scale and character of surrounding development? Should the new development seek to reinforce this?
- What locally distinctive architecture or townscape, reflecting the traditional materials and culture of the area, could be used as a starting-point for design?

THE DEVELOPMENT PROPOSAL IN CONTEXT

This section provides a checklist for evaluating the master plan or site plan stage of a project that follows the assessment. The master plan is concerned with defining the exact uses, the pattern of development on the site and how development ties into the surrounding area.

Depending on the scale of the development, the questions have a different significance. On very major sites with a range of uses and perhaps more than 1000 dwellings, the questions relate more to the internal arrangements. For smaller sites, the question is how they fit into the wider neighbourhood.

The mix of activities
- Does the development contribute to a broad pattern of mixed use, with a rough balance of homes, jobs and services in any given locality, township or small settlement?
- Does the development complement (rather than reproduce) the neighbouring activities and link to them by easy, direct access to enhance viability and attractiveness?
- If employment or services: does it avoid the creation of single-use or isolated facilities, instead contributing to clusters with mixed uses in local centres or high streets?
- If housing: does it provide options for home-based work or subsequent change of use to local services?

Housing balance
- Does the development contribute to ensuring a wide variety of types of housing (especially tenure and price) within a given neighbourhood or small town?
- If this is a large development (varies with the context; the official threshold in the United Kingdom is 25 dwellings), does it include a proportion of social housing?
- Again, if this is a larger project, does it provide variation on site in relation to gardens, built form and character to offer options to people with different needs?

Public transport access

- Is the land close to public transport used at an appropriately high intensity to facilitate access to public transport?
- If this is a major development: are the main magnets of pedestrian activity located close to tram or bus routes and every part of the development within striking distance (for example, 400 metres) of a stop?
- Are any stops financed by the development conveniently located near the main users, well served by pedestrian routes, sheltered, visible and safe?

Cycling

- Is the level of design appropriate to encourage potential cyclists?
- Do any cycle routes provided by the development link effectively with desire lines for the wider area?
- Are the cycle routes as direct as possible, with gradients, bends, curbs and junctions designed correctly?
- Have potential areas of conflict between cyclists and vehicles or pedestrians been identified and effectively resolved?
- Has provision been made (if appropriate) for secure cycle parking?

Pedestrian environment

- Do pedestrian routes create a continuous and coherent network ensuring a permeable environment with ease of access to all neighbouring areas?
- Are gradients and the use of kerbs minimized to facilitate use by people with impaired mobility such as elderly people, partially sighted people, wheelchair users and by parents with pushchairs and children with skateboards, roller skates or tricycles?
- Are the road-crossing points designed to give pedestrians the right of way wherever possible and effective protection from traffic?
- Are the footpaths designed to give visually attractive and varied routes while ensuring good visibility and minimal risk of ambush?
- Are the public faces of buildings turned towards footpaths and squares so that they provide informal surveillance?

Road traffic and parking

- Is there a legible road hierarchy that allows ease of access for vehicles and reasonably direct routes (to minimize noise and pollution) within and around the development?
- Are roads in residential, shopping and central areas designed for "natural" traffic calming, with 30 km/h design speed and priority for pedestrians, cyclists and buses clearly established?
- Is the number of parking spaces as low as is realistic given the use and the location of the development?

Public space
- Is provision made for accessible and appropriate open spaces – particularly satisfying local needs for meeting-places, leisure, cafés, children's play, kick-around activities, sport, allotment gardens and recreational walks?
- Are green spaces designed with both beauty and a sense of safety in mind?
- Does green space in the development link into a wider network:
  - encouraging circular walks and cycle rides?
  - providing a variety of wildlife habitats?
  - managing water resources sustainably?
  - managing the microclimate?
  - helping to control and reduce pollution?

Energy strategy
- Is the development designed to minimize the need for artificial heating or cooling, with appropriate solar orientation and natural ventilation?
- Has the landscape around the buildings been designed to reduce wind speed, provide summer shade and allow winter sun?
- Is the heating or cooling system (if needed) the most environmentally economical available: for example, in temperate climates, combined heat and power using renewable fuels?

Water strategy
- Does the proposed development catch and purify rainwater to provide for at least some uses on site?
- Are systems to be installed that encourage reuse of grey water?
- If the existing capacity in centralized sewage systems is limited or none is accessible, will the development deal with its own sewage?
- Will all surface water be allowed to percolate into the ground or reach local streams, with pollutants removed?

BUILDINGS AND PRIVATE SPACES

Privacy, security and gardens
- Does the layout of external spaces around homes provide an appropriate level of surveillance and sense of user control, clearly distinguishing between public and private access?
- In areas with lower density, are gardens shaped and oriented to assist home growing and composting?
- In areas with higher density, are there balconies, roof gardens or patios, or communal gardens or allotments next to the buildings?

Box 6.1. Master plan for a sustainable urban environment:
Oikos (the Netherlands)

Oikos is to be a part of a planned new suburb called The Eschmarke, an area to the east of Enschede and close to the German border within the Twente region of the Netherlands. The national government allocated the area as a location for housing development in accordance with the national housing policy (VINEX). The intention is to build 600 new solar-heated homes providing a mixture of dwelling types and social tenure and to incorporate the natural landscape features around a water system. The design of Oikos is based on a multidisciplinary approach and aims to create a living environment in which several sustainability aspects are integrated with human desires and needs. The intention is that the natural environment will be closer to the inhabitants, and they will be closer to nature and will therefore have more respect for the natural environment.

The first phase of the scheme for 250 dwellings commenced in spring 1994, and construction followed in August 1996 using a multidisciplinary project team with a specialist environmental consultant. The implementation of the project specified the use of sustainable building materials and products and required a signed commitment to ecologically sound principles. Existing water features and green spaces determined the urban design for the project and have been incorporated within the scheme for filtration and drainage purposes. Car access to the site has been allowed, but public transport and pedestrians and cyclists have been given priority. In addition, two new central green spaces have been designed as distinctive local features. Funding for the project resulted from the development of the land and the sale of the houses. The second phase of the project, for the development of a further 350 dwellings, started in 1997 and was almost completed in April 2000. A further 500 dwellings were being planned.

Chapter 1 highlights the key health objectives of urban planning. This case study fulfils the objectives of housing quality, accessibility and social cohesion. The municipality has found that the project has strengthened the cooperation between departments after initial problems due to professional differences among the project team. As a result, they have drawn up a list of recommendations for other municipalities planning similar schemes.

Source: EURONET/ICLEI Consortium *(81)*

Box 6.2.   The Povel experience: regeneration of contaminated
land in Nordhorn (Germany)

In 1979 Nordhorn, a medium-sized town in northwestern Germany, was faced
with an environmental and economic crisis when a large textile factory known
as Povel-van Delden shut down. Textile manufacturing had been the major
source of employment in the town since the end of the nineteenth century,
and the closure created a 15-hectare site adjoining the historical city centre.
Realizing this as an opportunity, the city acquired the land for development
in 1985 but discovered that the site was seriously contaminated when it
demolished the buildings.

This caused great alarm, and the city authorities set about consulting a
range of technical experts and developed a flexible strategy for removing
the waste. This was achieved without exporting any of the contaminated
waste to other regions and using a minimum of resources. The Povel model
of soil cleansing was developed as an ecologically sound solution to the
problem and has been in operation since 1987. This has allowed the town
renewal scheme to proceed, together with the creation of new employment
opportunities through private investment of more than DM 200 million. The
Povel project has been sponsored and supported by federal and Lower
Saxony authorities.

Chapter 1 highlighted the importance of retaining quality land and mineral
resources, and this example shows what can be achieved in areas where
there is the reverse situation of very high industrial contamination. It allows
redevelopment to contribute towards revitalizing declining urban areas.

Source: Together Foundation and United Nations Centre for Human Settlements (82)

Use of existing buildings and local materials
- Have existing buildings on site been incorporated in the development scheme?
- Have local sources of traditional building materials (normally associated with low energy use) been identified and used where appropriate, to give more of a sense of place and continuity with the past?

Noise and pollution
- Are the buildings laid out and constructed to minimize problems of noise between neighbours on and off site?
- Have problems of airborne pollution (from neighbouring areas), on-site ground contamination or watercourse pollution been identified and managed to reduce health risks to an acceptable level?

Chapter 7

Conclusions

A healthy approach to urban planning is needed. Issues of health, wellbeing and quality of life need to be considered during the urban planning process to resolve many of the problems faced in cities today. Unemployment, pollution, poor housing, inequity, poverty, unhealthy environments, lack of access to jobs, goods and services, stress and lack of community cohesion all affect people's health and wellbeing. Each of these can be influenced, in some form or another, by urban planning.

A healthy city is not a place created only for the needs of a healthy and active adult man. A healthy city is a place where pollution, crime, stress and unemployment are minimized and where all human beings can live a healthy and fulfilling life according to their needs, irrespective of their age, gender, race and physical or socioeconomic circumstances. A new model of urban planning, healthy urban planning, is needed to achieve such a city.

Some people believe that the need to follow "sound" urban planning policies that promote health and sustainable development and the need to improve the economy of the city are in conflict. The need to follow healthy urban planning policies could well be considered too costly, and the limitations of urban planning budgets too great to implement healthy urban planning. However, unhealthy urban planning imposes an increasing fiscal burden on health services, police services and social services and a general economic and social burden on individuals and companies. This means that the real issue is not how much it would cost to implement healthy urban planning but how much it costs every day not to implement it. Chronic disease, lack of social cohesion, unemployment and crime are all steadily increasing in most of Europe's cities. These problems are an enormous drain on the public purse, and healthy urban planning, along with other economic, social and environmental policies to promote health and sustainability, can provide a solution.

This book discusses the principles, processes, policies and practice of healthy urban planning. The themes discussed – including equity, intersectoral cooperation, community participation, sustainability and the links to Local Agenda 21, regeneration, urban form, neighbourhood, indicators and the assessment of health effects, accessibility and transport, public spaces, and housing – are all important in developing healthy urban planning.

Healthy urban planning (in a holistic sense) in European cities is still largely conceptual. In practical terms, many urban planners today work in "traditional" ways: disjointed sectoral activities, marginal projects and a short term view of effects, especially in relation to the economic benefits, are several examples. However, increasing numbers of cities are recognizing the links between health and urban planning and are taking steps to incorporate HEALTH21 and Healthy Cities principles into urban planning practices. In a few noteworthy cities, significant steps are being taken to promote healthy urban planning and to experiment with new ways of working familiar to the WHO Healthy Cities project. In these cities, increasing levels of collaboration between health and urban planning departments, not only for isolated projects but in a strategic way, are evidence of this.

WHO will have more to say and do on healthy urban planning in the future. This book comprises part of WHO's continuing initiative during the third phase of the Healthy Cities project (1998–2002), to emphasize the links between health and urban planning and to promote healthy urban planning across Europe.

The first WHO Seminar on Healthy Urban Planning, held in Milan, Italy, in October 1999, marked the beginning of this initiative. Its purpose was to explore how the Centre for Urban Health of the WHO Regional Office for Europe can best support healthy urban planning at the local level and to provide a forum for WHO and urban planners to discuss the issues. Urban planners from cities participating in the WHO European Healthy Cities network in northern, southern, eastern and western Europe were enthusiastic about this new area of work. Discussion focused on conceptual issues and case studies from cities already beginning to develop healthy urban planning. Many new ideas emerged from this Seminar, including that of a city action group, which would provide a continuing forum for cities to meet and exchange ideas and experience. The need for tools, concise information for policy-makers and further case studies was identified, and participants recognized their own role in this process, in particular with regard to piloting the guidelines suggested in this book. The need to promote healthy urban planning at both the national and international level was also highlighted.

Cities throughout Europe and beyond are invited and encouraged to become involved in healthy urban planning. The Web site of the WHO Healthy Cities project (http://www.who.dk/healthy-cities) provides up-to-date information on all the work of the WHO Centre for Urban Health, including the developmental work on healthy urban planning. It also provides access to many of the Healthy Cities books and documents cited here.

Urban planners and development professionals are called on to help progress the healthy urban planning initiative and to contribute to debate and practical implementation. Likewise, academics and students are called on to focus on the health implications of urban planning in their work, and universities are asked to include the concept of healthy urban planning in degree and other courses related to the urban environment. Healthy urban planning requires change to embrace the principles of HEALTH21 and the Healthy Cities movement. This book provides the stimulus and guidance needed to support that change.

References

1. EUROPEAN COMMISSION EXPERT GROUP ON THE URBAN ENVIRONMENT. *European sustainable cities* (http://europa.eu.int/comm/environment/urban/rport-en.pdf). Luxembourg, Office for Official Publications of the European Communities, 1994 (CR-17-98-863-EN-C) (accessed 30 May 2000).
2. DUHL, L.J. & SANCHEZ, A.K. *Healthy cities and the city planning process – a background document on links between health and urban planning* (http://www.who.dk/healthy-cities/hcppub.htm#Plan). Copenhagen, WHO Regional Office for Europe, 1999 (accessed 30 May 2000).
3. *Town planning and health.* Copenhagen, WHO Regional Office for Europe, 1997 (Local Authorities Health and Environment Briefing Pamphlet Series, No. 16).
4. *Contaminated land.* Copenhagen, WHO Regional Office for Europe, 1997 (Local Authorities Health and Environment Briefing Pamphlet Series, No. 17).
5. *Green cities, blue cities.* Copenhagen, WHO Regional Office for Europe, 1997 (Local Authorities Health and Environment Briefing Pamphlet Series, No. 18).
6. *The city of the future.* Copenhagen, WHO Regional Office for Europe, 1997 (Local Authorities Health and Environment Briefing Pamphlet Series, No. 27).
7. *Walking and cycling in the city.* Copenhagen, WHO Regional Office for Europe, 1997 (Local Authorities Health and Environment Briefing Pamphlet Series, No. 35).
8. *Towards a new planning process. A guide to reorienting urban planning towards Local Agenda 21* (http://www.who.dk/healthy-cities/hcppub.htm#book3). Copenhagen, WHO Regional Office for Europe, 1999 (document EUR/ICP/POLC 06 03 05C, European Sustainable Development and Health Series, No. 3) (accessed 30 May 2000).
9. NEWMAN, P. & THORNLEY, A. *Urban planning in Europe.* London, Routledge, 1996.
10. CIN, A.D. & LYDDON, D., ED. *International manual of planning practice.* The Hague, International Society of City and Regional Planners/Association internationale des urbanistes, 1992.

11. GREEN, G. *Health and governance in European cities: a compendium of trends and responsibilities for public health in 46 member states of the WHO European Region.* London, European Hospital Management Journal Ltd, 1998.

12. LALONDE, M. *A new perspective on the health of Canadians.* Ottawa, Health and Welfare Canada, 1974.

13. WHITEHEAD, M. & DAHLGREN, G. What can we do about inequalities in health. *The lancet,* **338**: 1059–1063 (1991).

14. LAUGHLIN, S. & BLACK, D., ED. *Poverty and health: tools for change.* Birmingham, Public Health Trust, 1995.

15. MARMOT, M. & WILKINSON, G., ED. *Social determinants of health.* Oxford, Oxford University Press, 1999.

16. WILKINSON, R. & MARMOT, M., ED. *The solid facts: social determinants of health* (http://www.who.dk/healthy-cities/hcppub.htm#SD). Copenhagen, WHO Regional Office for Europe, 1998 (document EUR/ICP/CHVD 03 09 01) (accessed 30 May 2000).

17. BARTON, H., ED. *Sustainable communities: the potential for eco-neighbourhoods.* London, Earthscan, 1999.

18. KUHL, D. & COOPER, C. Physical activity at 36 years: patterns and childhood predictors in a longitudinal study. *Journal of epidemiology and community health,* **46:** 114–119 (1992).

19. *Draft urban food and nutrition action plan* (http://www.who.dk/nutrition/pdf/ Urban99.pdf). Copenhagen, WHO Regional Office for Europe, 1999 (accessed 30 May 2000).

20. MCMICHAEL, A.J. ET AL., ED. *Climate change and human health: an assessment prepared by a Task Group on behalf of the World Health Organization, the World Meteorological Organization and the United Nations Environment Programme.* Geneva, World Health Organization, 1996 (document WHO/EHG/ 96.7).

21. LUKE, J. *Catalytic leadership: strategies for an interconnected world.* San Francisco, Jossey-Bass Publishers, 1998.

22. *Global strategy for health for all by the year 2000.* Geneva, World Health Organization ("Health for All" Series, No. 3).

23. *Health for all in the 21st century.* Geneva, World Health Organization, 1998 (document WHA 51/5).

24. *HEALTH21 – the health for all policy framework for the WHO European Region* (http://www.who.dk/cpa/h21/h21long.htm). Copenhagen, WHO Regional Office for Europe, 1999 (European Health for All Series, No. 6) (accessed 30 May 2000).

25. *Ottawa Charter for Health Promotion* (http://www.who.dk/policy/ottawa.htm). Copenhagen, WHO Regional Office for Europe, 1986 (accessed 30 May 2000).

26. *Agenda 21* (http://www.un.org/esa/sustdev/agenda21text.htm). New York, United Nations Division for Sustainable Development, updated 20 March 2000 (accessed 30 May 2000).

27. WORLD COMMISSION ON ENVIRONMENT AND DEVELOPMENT. *Our common future.* Oxford, Oxford University Press, 1987, p. 43.

28. *Rio Declaration on Environment and Development* (http://www.un.org/ documents/ga/conf151/aconf15126-1annex1.htm). New York, United Nations Department of Social and Economic Affairs, 12 August 1992 (accessed 30 May 2000).

29. PRICE, C. & DUBÉ, P. *Sustainable development and health: concepts, principles and framework for action for European cities and towns* (http://www.who.dk/ healthy-cities/hcppub.htm#sustdev). Copenhagen, WHO Regional Office for Europe, 1997 (document EUR/ICP/POLC 06 03 05a, European Sustainable Development and Health Series, No. 1) (accessed 30 May 2000).

30. *City planning for health and sustainable development* (http://www.who.dk/ healthy-cities/hcppub.htm#planning). Copenhagen, WHO Regional Office for Europe, 1997 (document EUR/ICP/POLC 06 03 05B, European Sustainable Development and Health Series, No. 2) (accessed 30 May 2000).

31. HANCOCK, T. & DUHL, L. *Promoting health in the urban context.* Copenhagen, FADL, 1988 (WHO Healthy Cities Papers, No. 1).

32. TSOUROS, A., ED. *World Health Organization healthy cities project: a project becomes a movement – review of progress 1987 to 1990.* Copenhagen, FADL and Milan, Sogess, 1990.

33. *WHO Healthy Cities project phase III: 1998–2002. The requirements and the designation process for WHO project cities* (http://www.who.dk/healthy-cities/ pdf/phase3e.pdf). Copenhagen, WHO Regional Office for Europe, 1997 (accessed 30 May 2000).

34. *Athens Declaration for Healthy Cities* (http://www.who.dk/healthy-cities/ hcppub.htm#Declaration). Copenhagen, WHO Regional Office for Europe, 1998 (document CHDV 03.01.01/BG3E) (accessed 30 May 2000).

35. HANCOCK, T. Planning and creating healthy and sustainable cities: the challenge for the 21st century. *In*: PRICE, C. & TSOUROS, A., ED. *Our cities, our future: policies and action plans for health and sustainable development* (http:// www.who.dk/healthy-cities/hcppub.htm#Our_Cities). Copenhagen, WHO Regional Office for Europe, 1996, pp. 65–88 (document EUR/ICP/HCIT 94 01/MT04(A)) (accessed 30 May 2000).

36. *City health planning: the framework.* Copenhagen, WHO Regional Office for Europe, 1996 (document EUR/ICP/HCIT 94 01/MT06/7).

37. ROGERS, R. *Cities for a small planet.* London, Faber and Faber, 1997.

38. *Community participation in local health and sustainable development: a working document on approaches and techniques* (http://www.who.dk/ healthy-cities/hcppub.htm#community). Copenhagen, WHO Regional Office for Europe, 1999 (document EUR/ICP/POLC 06 03 05D, European Sustainable Development and Health Series, No. 4) (accessed 30 May 2000).

39. DAVIDSON, S. Spinning the wheel of empowerment. *Planning*, issue 1262 (3 April): 14–15 (1998).

40. WATES, N. & KNEVITT, C. *Community architecture: how people are creating their own environment*. London, Penguin, 1987.

41. *Twenty steps for developing a Healthy Cities project* (http://www.who.dk/healthy-cities/hcppub.htm#Steps). 3rd ed. Copenhagen, WHO Regional Office for Europe, 1997 (document EUR/ICP/HSC 644(2)) (accessed 30 May 2000).

42. *Application for designation to phase III of the WHO Healthy Cities project*. Belfast, Belfast Healthy Cities, 1998.

43. *City health profiles – how to report on health in your city* (http://www.who.dk/healthy-cities/hcppub.htm#City_Health). Copenhagen, WHO Regional Office for Europe, 1995 (document ICP/HSIT/94/01 PB 02) (accessed 30 May 2000).

44. *City health profiles – a review of progress* (http://www.who.dk/healthy-cities/hcppub.htm#Profile). Copenhagen, WHO Regional Office for Europe, 1998 (document EUR/ICP/CHDV 03 01 01/1) (accessed 30 May 2000).

45. *Healthy city plan of the City of Copenhagen, 1994–1997*. Copenhagen, Healthy City Project, Copenhagen Health Services, 1994.

46. *Sharpening the focus on health: a city health development plan*. Stoke on Trent, Stoke on Trent Healthy City, 1999.

47. *National healthy cities networks*. 3rd ed. Copenhagen, WHO Regional Office for Europe, 1997 (document ICP/HSC 644).

48. *Guidelines for multi-city action plans – WHO Healthy Cities project, phase II 1993–1997* (http://whqlibdoc.who.int/euro/1994-97/EUR_ICP_HSC_640(B).pdf). Copenhagen, WHO Regional Office for Europe, 1994 (document EUR/ICP/HSC 640(B)) (accessed 30 May 2000).

49. *Healthy urban planning. Report on a WHO seminar, Milan, Italy, 17–18 October 1999* (http://www.who.dk/healthy-cities/meetmila.htm). Copenhagen, WHO Regional Office for Europe, 2000 (document EUR/ICP/CHDV 03 03 03) (accessed 30 May 2000).

50. TSOUROU, C. *Proceedings of a seminar on healthy urban planning organized by WHO, Milan, Italy, 17–18 October 1999*. Milan, Municipality of Milan, Healthy Cities Project Office, 2000.

51. TSOUROU, C. *Pianificazione urbanistica e salute implicazioni della stratega dell'oms "salute per tutti" nella pianificazione urbanistica in Europa* [Urban planning and health: implications of the WHO strategy for health for all for urban planning in Europe]. Thesis. Venice, Institute of Architecture, University of Venice, 1998.

52. HEALTHY CITY OFFICE. *Il progetto bambino urbano* [The urban child project]. Milan, City of Milan, 1996.

53. *Healthy Newcastle – our city application for designation, WHO Healthy Cities project, phase III 1998–2002*. Newcastle, Newcastle Health Partnership, 1998.

54. WASCHITZ, B. *The Jerusalem Association of Community Councils and Centers – a case study in democratization* (http://www.who.dk/healthy-cities/pdf/israel.pdf, pp. 5–8). Copenhagen, WHO Regional Office for Europe, 1998 (accessed 30 May 2000).

55. BARTON, H. ET AL. *Sustainable settlements: a guide for planners, developers and designers*. Bristol, University of the West of England and Luton, Local Government Management Board, 1995.

56. *Project Hammarby Sjöstad. A new district where technology meets ecology*. Stockholm, Stockholm Water Company, 1999.

57. BARTON, H. & BRUDER, N. *A guide to local environmental auditing*. London, Earthscan, 1995.

58. COMMISSION OF THE EUROPEAN COMMUNITIES. *Green paper on the urban environment*. Luxembourg, Office for Official Publications of the European Communities, 1990.

59. *Report on a technical meeting on transport and health, Udine, Italy*. Copenhagen, WHO Regional Office for Europe, 1999 (unit document, Centre for Urban Health).

60. *Implementation of human settlements policies on urban renewal and housing modernization – Vienna case study*. Geneva, United Nations Economic Commission for Europe, 1998 (ECE/HBP/106).

61. *Health principles of housing*. Geneva, World Health Organization, 1989.

62. *Report: Third Ministerial Conference on Environment and Health, London, 16–18 June 1999* (http://www.who.dk/london99/reporte.htm). Copenhagen, WHO Regional Office for Europe, 15 July 1999 (document EUR/ICP/EHCO 02 02 05/19) (accessed 30 May 2000).

63. *Charter on Transport, Environment and Health* (http://www.who.dk/london99/transporte.htm). Copenhagen, WHO Regional Office for Europe, 1999 (document EUR/ICP/EHCO 02 02 05/9 Rev.4) (accessed 30 May 2000).

64. CROWHURST-LENNARD, S.H. & LENNARD, H.L. *Livable cities*. Southampton, NY, Gondolier Press, 1987.

65. *ADONIS Project (Analysis and Development of New Insights into Substitution of Short Car Trips by Cycling and Walking). Summary of the ADONIS report*. Gentofte, Denmark, Danish Council of Road Safety Research, 1998.

66. *How to substitute short car trips by cycling and walking*. Gentofte, Denmark, Danish Council of Road Safety Research, 1997.

67. *Best practice to promote cycling and walking*. Copenhagen, Road Directorate, 1997.

68. MILLS, G. Fuel savings from park and ride schemes. *In*: FARTHING, S., ED. *Towards sustainability conference papers*. Bristol, Faculty of the Built Environment, University of the West of England, 1997, pp. 41–61 (Working Paper No. 38).

69. *Lyon Parc Auto, Lyon, France: integration of parking and urban policies* (http://www.cities21.com/egpis/egpc-048.html). Bristol and Freiburg, EURONET/ICLEI Consortium, 1996 (accessed 30 May 2000).

70. *Metropolitan Bilbao, Spain: strategic plan for the revitalisation of Metropolitan Bilbao* (http://www.cities21.com/egpis/egpc-052.html). Bristol and Freiburg, EURONET/ICLEI Consortium, 1996 (accessed 30 May 2000).

71. LYON, A. *Housing improvement, public health and the local economy: better housing, better health. In*: PRICE, C. & TSOUROS, A., ED. *Our cities, our future: policies and action plans for health and sustainable development* (http://www.who.dk/healthy-cities/hcppub.htm#Our_Cities). Copenhagen, WHO Regional Office for Europe, 1996, pp. 98–101 (document EUR/ICP/HCIT 94 01/MT04(A)) (accessed 30 May 2000).

72. *Project profile community heating: Glasgow, Hutchesontown*. London, Combined Heat and Power Association, 1998. and for further information

73. SCOTTISH HOMES. *Evaluation of energy efficiency measures at Hutchesontown multi-storey blocks* (http://www.scot-homes.gov.uk/pdfs/pubs/51.pdf). Edinburgh, Scottish Homes, 1999 (Precis Research Report No. 88) (accessed 30 May 2000).

74. *WHO guidelines for air quality, 1999* (http://www.who.int/peh/air/Airqualitygd.htm). Geneva, World Health Organization, 1999 (accessed 30 May 2000).

75. *The municipal plan of Horsens*. Horsens, Denmark, Municipality of Horsens, 1993.

76. *Handbook on neighbourhood planning: the Gasvej neighbourhood project, 1987–91*. Horsens, Denmark, Municipality of Horsens, 1991.

77. DEPARTMENT OF HEALTH. *Our healthier nation: a contract for health* (http://www.ohn.gov.uk/ohn/ohn.htm). London, The Stationery Office, 1998 (accessed 30 May 2000).

78. *Milton Keynes planning manual*. Milton Keynes, Milton Keynes Development Corporation, 1992.

79. HILLMAN, M. & WHALLEY, A. *Walking is transport*. London, Policy Studies Institute, 1979.

80. KLEINER, D. Innovative eco-neighbourhood projects. *In*: BARTON, H. ET AL., ED. *Sustainable settlements: a guide for planners, developers and designers*. Bristol, University of the West of England and Luton, Local Government Management Board, 1995, pp. 66–85.

81. *City of Enschede, the Netherlands: Oikos, suburban sustainable development of 600 houses in the east of the Netherlands, by the German border* (http://www.cities21.com/egpis/egpc-077.html). Bristol and Freiburg, EURONET/ICLEI Consortium, 1996 (accessed 30 May 2000).

82. *The Povel experience: a local solution for a global challenge – Germany* (http://www.bestpractices.org/cgi-bin/bp98.cgi?cmd=detail&id=147). New York and Nairobi, Together Foundation and United Nations Centre for Human Settlements, 1998 (accessed 30 May 2000).

HEALTH21: health for all targets for the European Region

Adopted by the WHO Regional Committee for Europe at its forty-eighth session, Copenhagen, September 1998

1 – Solidarity for health in the European Region: *By the year 2020, the present gap in health status between Member States of the European Region should be reduced by at least one third.*

2 – Equity in health: *By the year 2020, the health gap between socioeconomic groups within countries should be reduced by at least one fourth in all Member States, by substantially improving the level of health of disadvantaged groups.*

3 – Healthy start in life: *By the year 2020, all newborn babies, infants and pre-school children in the Region should have better health, ensuring a healthy start in life.*

4 – Health of young people: *By the year 2020, young people in the Region should be healthier and better able to fulfil their roles in society.*

5 – Healthy aging: *By the year 2020, people over 65 years should have the opportunity of enjoying their full health potential and playing an active social role.*

6 – Improving mental health: *By the year 2020, people's psychosocial wellbeing should be improved and better comprehensive services should be available to and accessible by people with mental health problems.*

7 – Reducing communicable diseases: *By the year 2020, the adverse health effects of communicable diseases should be substantially diminished through systematically applied programmes to eradicate, eliminate or control infectious diseases of public health importance.*

8 – Reducing noncommunicable diseases: *By the year 2020, morbidity, disability and premature mortality due to major chronic diseases should be reduced to the lowest feasible levels throughout the Region.*

9 – Reducing injury from violence and accidents: *By the year 2020, there should be a significant and sustainable decrease in injuries, disability and death arising from accidents and violence in the Region.*

10 – A healthy and safe physical environment: *By the year 2015, people in the Region should live in a safer physical environment, with exposure to contaminants hazardous to health at levels not exceeding internationally agreed standards.*

11 – Healthier living: *By the year 2015, people across society should have adopted healthier patterns of living.*

12 – Reducing harm from alcohol, drugs and tobacco: *By the year 2015, the adverse health effects from the consumption of addictive substances such as tobacco, alcohol and psychoactive drugs should have been significantly reduced in all Member States.*

13 – Settings for health: *By the year 2015, people in the Region should have greater opportunities to live in healthy physical and social environments at home, at school, at the workplace and in the local community.*

14 – Multisectoral responsibility for health: *By the year 2020, all sectors should have recognized and accepted their responsibility for health.*

15 – An integrated health sector: *By the year 2010, people in the Region should have much better access to family- and community-oriented primary health care, supported by a flexible and responsive hospital system.*

16 – Managing for quality of care: *By the year 2010, Member States should ensure that the management of the health sector, from population-based health programmes to individual patient care at the clinical level, is oriented towards health outcomes.*

17 – Funding health services and allocating resources: *By the year 2010, Member States should have sustainable financing and resource allocation mechanisms for health care systems based on the principles of equal access, cost–effectiveness, solidarity, and optimum quality.*

18 – Developing human resources for health: *By the year 2010, all Member States should have ensured that health professionals and professionals in other sectors have acquired appropriate knowledge, attitudes and skills to protect and promote health.*

19 – Research and knowledge for health: *By the year 2005, all Member States should have health research, information and communication systems that better support the acquisition, effective utilization, and dissemination of knowledge to support health for all.*

20 – Mobilizing partners for health: *By the year 2005, implementation of policies for health for all should engage individuals, groups and organizations throughout the public and private sectors, and civil society, in alliances and partnerships for health.*

21 – Policies and strategies for health for all: *By the year 2010, all Member States should have and be implementing policies for health for all at country, regional and local levels, supported by appropriate institutional infrastructures, managerial processes and innovative leadership.*

Cities participating in the WHO European Healthy Cities network in phases I, II and III

Country	Phase I (1987–1992)	Phase II (1993–1997)	Phase III (1998–2002)
Austria	Vienna	Vienna	Vienna
Belgium	Liège Mechelen	Liège Mechelen	
Croatia	Zagreb		Zagreb Rjeka
Czech Republic		Brno Sumperk	Brno
Denmark	Copenhagen Horsens	Copenhagen Horsens	Copenhagen Horsens
Estonia			Kuressaare
Finland	Turku	Turku	Turku
France	Rennes Nancy Montpellier	Rennes Nancy	Rennes
Germany	Dresden Frankfurt Bremen Düsseldorf Munich	Dresden Frankfurt	Dresden
Greece	Patras	Patras Athens	Athens
Hungary	Pécs	Pécs Györ	Pécs Györ
Ireland	Dublin	Dublin	Dublin
Israel	Jerusalem	Jerusalem	Jerusalem

Country	Phase I (1987–1992)	Phase II (1993–1997)	Phase III (1998–2002)
Italy	Milan Padua	Milan Padua Bologna	Milan Padua Bologna Arezzo Udine
Lithuania	Kaunas	Kaunas	
Netherlands	Eindhoven Rotterdam	Eindhoven Rotterdam	Rotterdam
Norway	Sandnes	Sandnes	Sandnes
Poland		Lodz Bialystock Poznan Torun	Lodz
Portugal		Amadora	Amadora Seixal
Russian Federation	St. Petersburg		Izhevsk
Slovakia		Kosice	Kosice
Slovenia		Maribor	Maribor
Spain	Barcelona Seville		San Fernando
Sweden	Gothenburg Stockholm	Gothenburg	Gothenburg Stockholm Helsingborg
Switzerland		Geneva	Geneva
United Kingdom	Belfast Camden Glasgow Liverpool	Belfast Camden Glasgow Liverpool	Belfast Camden Glasgow Liverpool Manchester Newcastle Sheffield Stoke on Trent
Total	34 cities	38 cities	41 cities

Some cities that participated in phase II were still going through the process of designation for phase III at the time of writing and are not shown under phase III.

Healthy Cities indicators during the second phase of the WHO Healthy Cities project (1993–1997)

This annex provides information on the 53 indicators used in the preparation of city health profiles during the second phase of the WHO Healthy Cities project (Chapter 2). These indicators were devised "to provide a baseline of information about cities, to characterize aspects of the health of the city populations which are unique to individual cities, and to allow for comparison of these aspects between cities".[1] Although these indicators have been revised down to a total of 32 for the third phase of the project, the original indicators are included in this book, as these were the ones that had been collected when WHO carried out its survey of urban planners at the end of the second phase (Chapter 3). Although the types of indicators currently used by urban planning departments may fall largely within the section on environmental indicators, this table shows that a wider range of indicators are relevant to healthy urban planning: A1–A3, B1, B5, B8, C1–C3, C6–C18, D1–D9, D13 and D20.

---

[1] WEBSTER, P. & PRICE, C., ED. *Healthy Cities indicators: analysis of data from cities across Europe* (http://www.who.dk/healthy-cities/hcppub.htm#Indic). Copenhagen, WHO Regional Office for Europe, 1997 (accessed 30 May 2000).

Number	Name	Definition	Method of calculation and unit of measurement	Frequency recommended by WHO
A. Health indicators				
A_1	Mortality: all causes	Annual mortality rate: all causes, according to age group	(No. of deaths/average population) times 100 000	Yearly
A_2	Cause of death	Annual mortality rate per cause of death studied. Code refers to International Classification of Diseases, 9th edition (ICD-9)	(No. of annual deaths per cause studied/average population) times 100 000	Yearly
A_3	Low birth weight	Percentage of children weighing 2.5 kg or less at birth	No. of children weighing less than 2.5 kg/no. of births	Yearly
B. Health service indicators				
B_1	Existence within the city of an inventory of self-help organizations	Indicate whether in the city or other health care boundary there is an inventory of self-help organizations or voluntary or non-profit-making organizations that are not part of the official care or social service system	Answer yes if there is an inventory, indicating the areas of action and the number of organizations concerned	Yearly
B_2	Existence within the city of a support programme for self-helporganizations	Support may be of a financial nature, in the form of human resources, or assistance of a different nature	Answer yes if there is an assistance structure, specifying the level of funding and, if relevant, the origin of funds (convert non-financial aid into money)	Yearly
B_3	Existence of a city health education programme	Programmes made up of one or several projects that aim to improve knowledge, assistance and services to individuals for developing and maintaining a healthy way of life	Answer yes or no specifying the project topic (smoking, diet, sexuality, etc.) and target groups	Yearly
B_4	Percentage of 6-year-old children fully immunized (having received all compulsory vaccinations)	Indicate the type of vaccine coverage given by the age of 6	(No. of 6-year-old children having received vaccination/no. of 6-year-old children) times 100	Yearly
B_5	Number of inhabitants per practising general practitioner	General practitioners are doctors who carry out their activity in the field of primary health care	Inhabitants living in the area/no. of general practitioners working in the area	Yearly

Number	Name	Definition	Method of calculation and unit of measurement	Frequency recommended by WHO
B6	Number of inhabitants per nurse	Nurses to be included are those working in the area(s) concerned, wherever they work (primary health, first aid services, generalist or specialist field)	Inhabitants living in the area/no. of full-time-equivalent nurses working in the area	Yearly
B7	Percentage of population covered by health insurance	Indicate people who have health insurance, if possible by the type: public or private, etc.	(Inhabitants living in the area covered by health insurance/no. of inhabitants living in the area) times 100	Yearly
B8	Percentage of the population having access to an emergency medical service that is less than 30 minutes away by car		(Estimated number of inhabitants living in the area living less than 30 minutes by car from the nearest emergency medical service/inhabitants living in the area) times 100	Yearly
B9	Availability of primary health care services in foreign languages	Indicate the availability of primary health care services where ethnic minority languages that are significantly representative in the city are spoken	Description of significant language groups and types of primary care services offered in the languages (% per language and services)	Yearly
B10	Health information communication	Existence of media (written, electronic, exhibitions or events) managed by the city that deal with social, sanitary or environmental aspects of health	Describe methods and use quantitative information: for example, number, volume, duration or frequency	Yearly
B11	Number of health questions examined by the city council every year	"Health questions" are those asked directly by the elected representatives of health, social and environmental services or departments	Specify the number of questions subdivided into these two categories	Yearly

C. Environmental indicators

Number	Name	Definition	Method of calculation and unit of measurement	Frequency recommended by WHO
C1	Atmospheric pollution	Parameters considered: sulfur dioxide, nitrogen dioxide, carbon monoxide, ozone, lead and dust (based on WHO guidelines for air quality)	For sulfur dioxide, dust and lead, indicate the number of days per year above the limit/total number of days per year with validated measurements	Yearly

Number	Name	Definition	Method of calculation and unit of measurement	Frequency recommended by WHO
			For nitrogen dioxide, carbon monoxide and ozone, indicate the number of hours per year above the limit/total number of days per year with validated measurements	
C_2	Microbial quality of the water supply	Percentage of measurements exceeding the recommended WHO guidelines	Number of measurements exceeding zero faecal coliforms per 100 ml/total number of measurements	Yearly
C_3	Chemical quality of the water supply	This indicator should show the chemical quality of the water distributed by the city	The rate at which the WHO guidelines are exceeded for nitrates, fluorine, benzene and chlordane/total number of measurements	Yearly
C_4	Percentage of water pollutants removed from total sewage produced	This indicator aims to show the quality of water purification before disposal	Percentage of pollutants removed	Yearly
C_5	Household waste collection quality index	It shows the quality of the collection in relation to the types of collecting systems used	Result as category – choose from: 0: loose; 1: in plastic bags; 2: in a sealed container; 3: voluntary selective collection; 4: home selective collection (% per category)	Yearly
C_6	Household waste treatment quality index	It shows the type of treatment used for household waste	Result as a category – choose from: 0: rough landfill; 1: sanitary landfill; 2: incineration without heat recovery; 3: incineration with heat recovery; 4: composting; 5: sorting centre, recycling (% per type)	Yearly
C_7	Pollution level indicator as perceived by the population	This indicator should give an idea of the nature and degree of pollution as perceived by the population (noise, smell, cleanliness)	By means of a study, based on a scale of 1 to 10 for each parameter	At least every 3 years

Number	Name	Definition	Method of calculation and unit of measurement	Frequency recommended by WHO
C_8	Quantity of drinking-water used per inhabitant per day	It should explain individual water consumption	Total no. of litres invoiced to households per day/no. of inhabitants	Yearly
C_9	Relative surface area of green spaces in the city	Gives an idea of the amount of vegetation in the city	Total surface area of green spaces in the city/ total surface area of the city (%)	Yearly
C_{10}	Public access to green spaces	The surface area per inhabitant of green spaces open to the public	Total no. of m^2 of green spaces with public access/no. of inhabitants	Yearly
C_{11}	Derelict industrial sites	Derelict industrial sites as a percentage of the total surface area of the city	(Surface area of derelict industrial sites/total surface area of the city) times 100	Yearly
C_{12}	Sport and leisure	Number of sports facilities per 1000 inhabitants	(Total no. of facilities/total population) times 1000	Yearly
C_{13}	Pedestrian streets	Shows the importance accorded to pedestrian streets	Total length of pedestrian streets/surface area of city (km/km^2)	Yearly
C_{14}	Cycling in the city	Shows the importance accorded to cycle paths	Total length of paths reserved for cyclists/ surface area of city (km/km^2)	Yearly
C_{15}	Public transport	Number of seats on public transport per 1000 inhabitants	(Average daily number of seats/total population) times 1000	Yearly
C_{16}	Public transport network coverage	Number of km served by public transport compared to the total no. of km of streets in the city	(Total km served by public transport/total km of streets) times 100	Yearly
C_{17}	Living space	Average number of rooms per inhabitant (rooms > 4 m^2, sanitary services not included)	Total number of rooms/no. of inhabitants	Yearly
C_{18}	Comfort and hygiene	Percentage of dwellings without a bathroom	No. of dwellings without a bathroom/total no. of dwellings (%)	Yearly
C_{19}	Emergency services	Fire service and other emergency services (emergency medical services)	No. of persons and vehicles per 1000 inhabitants	Yearly
D. Socioeconomic indicators				
D_1	Number of square metres of living space per inhabitant	Living space per inhabitant in each district, or part of city	Total living space within district/total no. of inhabitants within district (m^2/inhabitant)	Every 5 years

Number	Name	Definition	Method of calculation and unit of measurement	Frequency recommended by WHO
D$_2$	Percentage of population living in substandard dwellings	Dwellings that do not fulfil the following requirements: • exclusive use of toilet and bath or shower • tap water inside the dwelling	(No. of inhabitants in substandard housing conditions in the area/no. of inhabitants in the area) times 100 (%)	Every 5 years
D$_3$	Estimated number of homeless people	No. of people having no housing (not including people who live in mobile homes)	Suggestion: data to be collected concerning assistance given to the homeless (no. of inhabitants)	Yearly
D$_4$	Unemployment rate	Percentage of working population that is unemployed	(Population unemployed/working population) times 100	
D$_5$	Working absenteeism rate	No. of days per year not worked for health reasons, compared to the total number of worked days per year	No. of days per year not worked for health reasons/no. of worked days per year (%)	
D$_6$	Percentage of families below the national poverty level	The national poverty threshold varies from country to country	No. of households living under the national poverty level/no. of households in the same area (%)	Yearly
D$_7$	Percentage of total employment provided by the ten most important economic activities		For each of the ten areas of economic activity: (no. of jobs in the economic sector/total no. of jobs in the same area) times 100 (%)	Every 5 years
D$_8$	Percentage of one-person households	Household: occupants of main residence, whether related or not, and may be made up of just one person	(Number of households of one person/ total number of households) times 100 (%)	Yearly
D$_9$	Percentage of single-parent families	A single parent and any unmarried children under 18 years	(Number of single-parent families/total number of families) times 100 (%)	Yearly
D$_{10}$	Percentage of children leaving school after compulsory education	N(A) : No. of pupils at school during their last year of compulsory education N(A+1): No. of pupils at school during the year following their last year of compulsory education	N(A)−N(A+1)/N(A) times 100(%)[a]	Yearly
D$_{11}$	Illiteracy rate	The fact of being unable to master reading or writing in the official language of the country of residence	Studies, estimates, specify origin of data in comments	Yearly

[a]The method of calculation for this indicator was incorrect in the original documents.

Number	Name	Definition	Method of calculation and unit of measurement	Frequency recommended by WHO
D_{12}	Percentage of city's budget allocated to health and social actions		(Percentage of city's budget allocated to health and social actions/total city budget) times 100 (% and amount in local currency)	Yearly
D_{13}	Crime rate	Definitions of crime vary. Please give some descriptive information about the definitions used in the city as well as survey information on the crime rate	(Number of offences/number of inhabitants) times 1000	Yearly
D_{14}	Percentage of dwellings for elderly people that have emergency call facilities	Percentage of residences housing people aged over 65 years equipped with a tele-alarm system	(No. of residences housing people aged over 65 equipped with emergency system/no. of residences housing people aged over 65) times 100 (%)	Yearly
D_{15}	Main causes for emergency calls	All telephone calls received by the main 24-hour emergency services (police, fire brigade, ambulance, the Samaritans, assistance for mistreated children, town hall, etc.)	According to cause for call: total number of calls recorded by each organization in given time period (no. and % per cause)	Yearly
D_{16}	Percentage of young children on waiting lists for child care facilities	Percentage of children below compulsory schooling age (under 6 in France), for whom a request for them to be taken charge of by a child care family, whether public or private (crèche, child minder, etc.) has not met with a positive answer	(No. of children on waiting lists for child care facilities/(number of children on waiting lists + number of children accepted)) times 100 (%)	Yearly
D_{17}	Median age of women giving birth for the first time	Median age of women at first birth (not first pregnancy)	Cumulative population of each age group (for example, in months), until half of the total population is reached (years + months)	Yearly
D_{18}	Abortion rate in relation to total number of births	Percentage of total number of abortions and miscarriages in relation to total number of births	(No. of abortions/no. of births) times 100 (%)	Yearly
D_{19}	Percentage of people under 18 "under police surveillance"	Refer to court orders for juveniles for: detention, probation, surveillance or similar judicial measures	(No. of people under 18 "under police surveillance"/no. of people under 18) times 100 (%)	Yearly

Number	Name	Definition	Method of calculation and unit of measurement	Frequency recommended by WHO
D_{20}	Percentage of disabled people in employment compared to total number of disabled people of working age (18–65 years)	Includes people in protected workshop (remunerated or not remunerated) able through their activity to participate in economic activity	(No. of disabled people in employment/total no. of disabled people in the same age range) times 100 (%)	Yearly

E. General information

For each population unit studied (part of the city, city, suburbs, etc.), respondents were asked to indicate the following demographic and social and occupational data:

- Year of census
- Total population
- Population according to sex
- Population according to age (0–1, 2–4, 5–9, 10–14, 15–19, 20–24, 25–29, 30–34, 35–39, 40–44, 45–49, 50–54, 55–59, 60–64, 65–69, 70–74, 75–79, 80–84, 85 or more years)
- Population in education (primary, secondary (aged 11–14), secondary (aged 15–18), university)
- Professional category (senior executives, liberal professions, employees, manual workers, homemakers)
- Surface area of population unit

Index